DON'T THINK ABOUT DEATH

DON'T THINK ABOUT DEATH

GARY LADERMAN

Deeds Publishing | Athens

Published by Deeds Publishing in Athens, GA
www.deedspublishing.com

Printed in The United States of America

Cover design by Mark Babcock. Text layout by Matt King.

ISBN 978-1-950794-12-6

Books are available in quantity for promotional or premium use. For information, email info@deedspublishing.com.

First Edition, 2020

10 9 8 7 6 5 4 3 2 1

This book is dedicated to the ghosts in my life.

Contents

Acknowledgements

Acknowledgements this time around are easy, given the nature of the book and my stage in life. This is all me, basically, and I put it together on my own and for myself. On the other hand, and upon deeper reflection, it is quite clear that nothing is as easy as it seems, and while the book is all me, I am more than just me, and important people in my life significantly contribute to everything I am and do, and therefore should be acknowledged here.

My two sons, Miles and Graham, inspire me by their talents, generosity, and incredible warmth and love. Their band, Hardcastle, currently provides much of the music to the soundtrack of my life. You will not find two better individuals. My wife, Liz, as you will read, is pivotal in my life and I certainly would not be doing what I'm doing without her and her family, the Hardcastle's. And speaking of family, where would I be without my mom and dad, Carol and Pete? Not here, that's for sure. My mom, as you will read, is no longer here in the flesh but here in everything I am. My dad remains a great friend, role model, and source of love in my life — ninety-one years old as I write these words. My brother, Dave, and his family, are always in my thoughts, and Dave is my close friend and advisor, and a remarkable soul-brother.

In addition to family, a small group of incredibly smart people should be noted who have been integral to my professional and personal development, though as I've gotten older I don't listen to their advice as much as I should. They are super friends who somehow for some reason continue to put up with me: Jill Peterson Adams, Paul Courtright, Sheila Davaney, Jeffrey Lesser, Jeff Morgen, Dave Orleans, Bobbi Patterson, Jill Robbins, Larry Schapiro, Steve Tipton, and Sally West, MD. You will read about how much Richard Hecht has done for me—I can honestly say without him I would not be writing these words. And finally, Michael Elliott, the Dean of Emory College of Arts and Science, is a close friend and a faculty member's dream: supportive, good-natured, and conscientious.

Finally, on the publishing journey, thanks very much to Jeffrey Goldman who helped along the way, and a word of gratitude to the folks at Deeds Publishing, and especially Bob Babcock for your fine work and strong commitments in the production of this book. Glad we found each other.

—November, 2019

Introduction

Books by experts on death are being published left and right. Doctors write on the topic frequently, funeral directors, too. The public eats up these books, because so many Americans can't stop thinking about death and want to learn about it, reflect on it, and understand how to live with it better. Death specialists, like funeral directors, and minor social media celebrities in their own right, Caitlin Doughty and Caleb Wilde, are two recent examples of successful literary undertakers; on the medical side, there are many examples, such as Atul Gawande's brilliant *Being Mortal*, or palliative care doctor, BJ Miller's playful and wise co-authored book (with Shoshana Berger), *A Beginner's Guide to the End*.

Who counts as an expert on mortal matters, and what counts as evidence for this crucial cultural authority, varies from society to society through human history. In ancient Egypt, the funerary priests had intimate expert knowledge of the dead, in the tombs and beyond them. Stories about certain deities in the Greco-Roman worlds, such as Charon or Thanatos, taught humans valuable lessons surrounding the details of death. Many indigenous cultures around the world include shamans, "masters in the arts of ecstasy" according to some, who can visit the worlds of the dead and return with important wisdom for the living community about death, and life. With monotheism, of course, there is only one true master of death, the one and only true God, and only He knows the truth of its meaning, purpose, and outcome. The Expert of experts. The separate and intertwined stories of Judaism, Christianity, and Islam, and all their various offshoots, is in part the story of how followers and founders have understood and interpreted His designs on human death.

In more modern times, two very different types of cultural authorities with their own intimate knowledge of death emerged and dramatically transformed the human experience with death: doctors and funeral directors. At first glance these historically male-dominated professions might seem obviously secular, and "different" in the sense of not being rooted in religious cosmologies. But even their revealed mysteries and authoritative proclamations derived from a peculiar familiarity with dead bodies are grounded in sacred assumptions, values, and rituals that teach the rest of us about the reality of death.

I have written a book on death from a different angle of expertise. This book tackles the subject through the lens of my life as a professor in the humanities, which has been unusually focused on death. As someone who has written two books and multiple essays and articles on the history of death in America, teaches courses on death and dying regularly, is frequently contacted by journalists and media outlets covering the subject, and has given public talks and interviews over the years, I have acquired my own fairly intimate, though definitely academic, knowledge of the topic in history and cultures. But now as an older man who is increasingly and frequently experiencing the reality of death in my personal life, the limits, and value, of that knowledge are becoming remarkably clear.

This book presents an unconventional take on how we live with death—or try to live with it at least. It is spurred, in part, by a recurring question that students and others ask me all the time: "Why do you think so much about death?" An inordinate amount of attention to mortality is obvious in some professions. We know why doctors write about it; it is obvious why funeral directors do too; even poets are supposed to write and think about death (the unique poet-funeral director Thomas Lynch does both, beautifully). But a humanities professor who is free to play in the fields of the liberal arts and plants his scholarly flag on death and dead bodies does seem to be a bit out of the ordinary, I admit.

The title refers to my earliest memory of death, after my grandfather had a heart attack and died in our bathtub when I was a young boy, and our rabbi discussed the meaning of death with me in the backyard. He told me not to think about death, and that life was for the living. The irony of course is that that religious counsel set me on a life course obsessing about death. The other irony I am hoping to capture with the title, and which is an important theme in the book, plays off the assumption that ours is a culture that denies death, or that it is still something of a "taboo" subject. My point is the opposite: Americans can't stop thinking about death.

Or maybe it's just me.

This book attempts to explain why I study death and to recall how I got to, and stuck with, the topic. It is divided in two. Part one consists of stories about death in my life, and how I veered into an academic career focusing on the cultural and historical analysis of death. It is personal, and short—not the whole story of my life, but focused laser-like on mortality as the primary thread in my development and aging. Part two consists of some of my published writings on death, both in academic, formal scholarly terms with peer-reviewed, but fun, journal articles, and as a public scholar with fun, but also serious, online essays. I don't think this kind of side by side display—personal stories and intellectual product—has ever been tried, but I could be wrong. The idea of this juxtaposition struck me as novel yet also potentially illuminating, and as a public scholar who thinks about ways to confound or transgress the boundaries between academic life and various publics, it is worth a try. The two parts together will, I hope, provide readers with food for thought about death in my life, and in your own.

Part One: Memories

1.

Introducing Death and Me

"Don't think about death."

One night when I was a young boy, my brother and I heard a commotion down the hall of our home. It was that surreal moment when you're suddenly awakened from a deep sleep and, for a second or two, it is not clear what is real and what is a dream. For a second I thought it was an earthquake. But soon enough, both me and my brother were in our bunkbeds, him on the bottom, me on the top, with our heads where our feet were supposed to be, looking out our door and down the hallway that seemed a million miles long but was, in reality, only twenty feet from one end to the other.

Firemen were running down that hallway and into our bathroom. That bathroom, in our three-bedroom, one bath house in the San Fernando Valley, was not big and yet, in that moment, I saw several firemen go in and out of it in what seemed a blink of an eye. Then I saw the reason for all this commotion. My grandfather, Zeda we called him, was being carried out on a stretcher by the firemen, dripping wet from the bath he had just entered. He had a heart attack and died in our bathtub.

I don't remember many of the repercussions from that evening—not what my father must have been feeling now that his father was no longer alive; not what my brother thought of the scene and his interpretation of what happened; not how my mother must have helped my father cope with his grief. No, the only thing I remember from that time, vivid and clear as if it occurred only yesterday, was a brief exchange with the rabbi who came to our house and spoke with me in our backyard soon after the death, but before the funeral.

Our discussion didn't last long, and the rabbi, who was a loved and respected leader of the Reform Jewish temple we attended, talked with me, a boy of eight, as if I was an adult. He was more intellect than emotion, and to be honest, I'm not sure what would have been more effective in giving me the tools to understand this situation, and its aftermath. I liked and respected this rabbi quite a bit.

For good or ill, he wanted me to think rather than emote, and asked, "Do you understand the meaning of death?" Of course I couldn't comprehend the question, and had no idea what to do or think, so had to reply, "No, no I don't."

"We all must face death, but God also ensures our immortality," he said. "We should take comfort in that and draw from it to help those who survive the death of a loved one. This will be a difficult time for your parents and they will need our love and support. Don't think about death. Life is better focused on the living, taking care of each other and planning for the future."

I was sitting on our little backyard picnic table, and the rabbi was standing next to me. I'm not sure if my brother was there too, though in my memory the zone of focus—his familiar and learned face, his eyes locked in on mine—did not include any others who may or may not have been with us then. How it ended, what else I may have said, are not within my grasp anymore. It was a transfixing moment, an exchange that now looking back, is pivotal and formative to the subsequent path my life would take. I was a marked man.

Rather than heed the good rabbi's advice, I defied it—not sure I could have done anything different even if I wanted to—and thought about death. A lot.

Who doesn't think a lot about death? If you don't now, you will, and if you think you can somehow avoid engaging with death, forget about it. We all know the bottom line so well it's engrained in clichés and prosaic sentiments: all that lives will die, to everything there is a season, the circle of life, and so on. Young people have certain intimations and experiences with death that bring it to mind, and older people can't keep it out of mind.

I am getting closer and closer to 60 and am intimately aware of the presence of death in life, having recently lost my mom, and currently living close to the edge with my dad, who is now over 90. Like many of my fellow Baby Boomers, my knowledge of and encounters with death, especially concerning aging and dying parents, is now increasingly part and parcel of daily living and awareness, and impacts not only my relations with others I love, but also my own self-understanding as a mortal being.

You would think I, of all people, would be especially prepared for life's inevitable end. After all, someone who spent his entire graduate program and professional career up close and personal with death, who has been teaching a college course on death for twenty or so years, and who has written numerous books and essays on the topic, must know and understand the ins and outs of the final passage better than most, and be more prepared when death does arrive, right? I can honestly say, when you get right down to it, the answer is "hell, no."

But believe me, I have tried for a long, long time to answer the rabbi from my childhood about the meaning of death. The truth is, I thought the challenge to understand it was intellectual—in my case, in the form of an historical analysis of death in America—but the visceral, spiritual, personal, emotional dimensions of my mom's death clarified what I had suspected all along: the existential lessons that come with losing

5

someone so close are of a different order than mere intellectual, academic engagement with the historical and cultural lessons learned from the study of death.

When I was a kid, contact with death was often minimal, obscure, and removed from the normal, quotidian social world I lived in during my childhood to teenage years in the San Fernando Valley. Pets died, so did grandparents, both making a great impact on me and young Baby Boomers generally who often had their first experience with death under one or both of those circumstances. On the other hand, death is not ever limited to the bosom of domestic family life. The world is often violent and cruel and unjust, and those intrusions into youth consciousness can be deeply impressionable. As an eighth grader, for example, I had one of the most jarring and traumatic encounters with death in my life, a memory still alive in my consciousness today, of a young girl who had just been hit by a van crossing the street next to our school.

I came upon the scene just after the accident. It was difficult to get a view, something I and just about every other student wanted after the accident. But as I got closer when the police and ambulance showed up, something changed and it struck me in my gut that I didn't really want to see the body, so turned back around and walked away. I did however get a glimpse of lots of the blood on the street, something horrific and frightening and compelling for some primal reasons I couldn't begin to understand then, or really even now. As I remember it, there was even the smell of death in the air, and the presence of death then and there left a multi-sensory impression on me.

Most of us don't usually see corpses on the streets and aren't used to the sight of dead people outside of their usual, more appropriate locations—in hospitals or funeral homes. Death is recognizable in these institutions, spaces which have contributed to a new way to approach death, to make death both real and familiar, in modern America. Their rise and dominance in American history are curiously parallel in many ways, and both together have altered how Americans in the twentieth century experienced death and related to the dead.

As a teenager in the 1970s, the worlds of hospitals and funeral homes opened up to me through the dying and death of my other grandparents, the one full of mysteries and miracles, the other creepier and more cryptic in its impressions on me. Still, even in these settings I felt removed from death, aware of its finality and impact, but not really thinking about it as an immediate concern with any great import, but something that comes with getting old, or by way of bad luck or unfortunate accidents for those not old. My other three grandparents died in hospitals, two from cancer and one after a car accident. At that stage of life, I had absolutely no clue about the excruciating details of bodily deterioration that comes with advanced aging in all three cases nor the medical efforts to save their lives as they lay dying. I was there for my parents, concerned about them and wanting but not knowing how to comfort them.

Visits to the funeral home, on the other hand, provided a very different milieu for encounters and interactions with death. One memory in particular often comes to mind when someone asks, "why did you start studying death?" I was a bit older when my mom's mother died, so played a minor role in her final disposition by carrying the casket from the hearse to the chapel in the Jewish funeral home where the ceremony would be taking place. After we put the casket on a stand, behind a curtain in the room, the funeral director and rabbi gathered the immediate family and opened the top half of the casket to reveal my embalmed, nicely dressed, peaceful looking grandmother inside. Without skipping a beat, as soon as I saw her there, I bent over and kissed her forehead, completely on impulse and without forethought. And it felt deep inside like the right thing to do.

It was a few minutes after that I tasted some makeup on my lips and realized there was in fact a ton of cosmetics used on her face. I don't think I really even knew what embalming was, or if it was in fact

7

announced by the funeral director when the casket was opened. This, I look back and am now sure, was a kernel, a seed, that was planted right then and there. It set the stage for what would later become the driving question of my dissertation and first book: where did embalming come from and how did it become so pervasive in America?

But at the time, I was mainly concerned with getting that taste out of my mouth and getting the ceremony over with, since for most of my life I have been unable to sit still for too long, and especially felt uncomfortable in anything resembling religious ritual.

So where else might a teenager from the San Fernando Valley in the late 1970s encounter death with a day to day life devoted to getting high, hanging with guy friends, and especially hanging with girl friends? Our family had stopped going to temple after my Bar Mitzvah, so death in its biblical senses was not really at play. I was in school but not really of school, then. Learning about death in literature or biology or world history didn't really grab my attention and I didn't see, as I do now, how saturated each is with the topic.

The great teacher of my time, of our time, who provides all of us with religious lessons about how to handle and what to believe about death, is not a prominent leader of a religious tradition nor a particular sacred scripture that holds sway over American society. No, the sacred source of authority on all matters, grand or small, grave or inspiring, in America, is popular culture. And popular culture instructs us in the realities of dying, death, and the afterlife, much as Christianity taught and shaped the meanings of death for many Europeans throughout Europe in the Middle Ages.

Forget about Jesus and the teachings of the New Testament after the 1960s. What really got the religious juices flowing were events like the spiritual return of Obi Wan Kenobi in *Star Wars*; the popular religious revivals of fans in the wake of Elvis's death; or the publication of Raymond Moody's popular book on near-death experiences, *Life After Life*.

Death was familiar and integrally present in popular cultures in the second half of the twentieth century, and in my little world, shared by many in the Baby Boom generation and beyond, music became an increasingly vital vehicle for the popular, public contemplation of mortality and morality, time and eternity, and body and spirit.

Kansas' "Dust in the Wind," or The Rolling Stones, "Dancing with Mr. D," or Blue Oyster Cult's, "Don't Fear the Reaper," or Prince's "Sign O' The Times." The list of songs referencing death, struggling with the meaning of death, playing with the idea of death, is endless, especially if you look across popular genres of music in the 70s, 80s, and 90s. No doubt the theme of death in music continues through the present moment, and can be found, I imagine, across global cultures and far into the past when humans began to make music.

Death in music, but also the deaths of musical legends made mortality a reality for me back then, in a removed yet powerful way. In most cases, these were unexpected deaths, not dying after a long life, so the lessons were often about drugs and fame, the search for fulfillment and the realization that life is full of absurdity and tragedy. When news broke of John Lennon's assassination and death in 1980, me and my high school friend Jeff Morgen were in a record store, stunned into silence like other customers when it was announced, confused and bewildered at such a seemingly random act of brutality. Another moment seared into consciousness.

So, like in all ages and at all times, it was hard for me to avoid death, even if I wasn't really consciously thinking about it all the time, nor experiencing it within the family circle.

A dream from the unconscious, however, clearly and unequivocally brought death home to me when I was in my early 20s. Do dreams have any special meaning or significance, or bring unique insights into the nature of personality or the cosmos? I don't think so, though some of them can be damn vivid and make a mark on you, as this one did on me.

In the dream it is night and I am on a Los Angeles freeway. The freeway lights are off, my car lights are off, and it is pitch black. I'm driving super-fast and dodging stopped cars as I'm going, noticing that all the other cars on the freeway are stalled and abandoned. For some reason, I'm sitting on the roof, holding on to the steering wheel outside the vehicle, my foot not on the accelerator but that doesn't seem to matter. I'm driving and dodging and very quickly realizing I will hit one of these abandoned autos soon, and that I will die. And that is what happens next.

I slam directly into a stalled car and at the moment of impact I am thrown from the car, projected into the air like a circus clown blown out of a cannon. Except I do not follow the laws of gravity and fall back to the cold hard dark concrete of the freeway. Instead, I start to ascend.

Now I should note that I, like many people, had heard the superstitious lore about what happens if you die in a dream. If you die in your dream, you'll have a heart attack in real life and croak. That's why you always wake up before you hit the ground when you're falling in dreams. At least that was my mindset at the time, going into the dream state during my afternoon nap as a young adult.

I was surprised when I didn't hit the ground and die in the dream, very conscious of not dying as I flew upward into the night sky, increasingly accelerating as I left earth's atmosphere and entered outer space. I should note that during this ascension to the heavens, my skin began to peel off, my limbs began to breakaway, and, in a surprisingly visceral experience for a dream, I lost my body.

What was left? Where did I go? The dream ends strangely. I am both a beam of light bouncing off the walls of a box with other light beams, all of which are familiar to me, and I am also outside of the box, observing it and aware of its contents.

Then I woke up, in a flash, and felt like I had just been given some kind of profound vision about myself, and the universe. The fact that I was still alive, that I had lived through a kind of death, was exhilarating and extraordinary to me at the time—it felt religious without being connected to any religion, a spiritual insight that was compelling in a unique way to me, different than other compelling experiences in my life at the time tied to hedonism, drugs, and music.

That experience with death, along with losing grandparents as a younger kid, aroused a curiosity about death that gradually bubbled to the surface in my mid-20s and set me on this peculiar morbid track. I say gradually because the not-so-slow transition from adolescent to young adult in the years between 18 and mid-20s were full of life, which at the time was defined for me in a very simple, clichéd, and pervasive mantra to live by, and alluded to above: sex, drugs, and rock and roll. Death? Not really relevant to those words of wisdom for me at the time, though the occasional celebrity overdose, the rise and spread of HIV/AIDS, and the fascinating macabre fixations in popular culture intruded on the purely hedonistic sensibilities driving my young adult self.

In the heady, high flying era of the early 1980s, a rather radical shift occurred that set my life in a starkly different direction than the road I was on—after high school I thought I'd try acting, continue working in record stores, and live the good life as I understood it then. It should come as no surprise that the radical shift was primarily the result of one person, a woman who set me on a different life path, and simultaneously opened up a surprising love for learning—I had no idea it was in me. Surprising and strange, given the history of my life as a student in public school which consisted primarily of me finding ways to hang with friends, be popular with girls, and get by with grades of Bs and Cs. For the most part, learning was not the priority through high school, but after attending city college, dropping out a couple of times, transferring to San Francisco State University and then to California State University, Northridge, in my junior year, it became evident to me that I wanted to spend my life as a student.

At the heart of my interests, and the one topic that drew me in and intrigued me to no end, was death. In psychology classes I became enamored with Sigmund Freud and "Thanatos," or the death instinct. I read Ernest Becker's brilliant *The Denial of Death*, studied Elizabeth Kübler-Ross's stages of grief, and immersed myself in other death classics in the field. In fact, I found that in most of the courses I was taking, in Philosophy, History, Literature, and Biology, the theme was omnipresent and unavoidable. I wasn't thinking about my death, or to prepare for the inevitable deaths of my family and friends, at least on any conscious level. For me, the intellectual stimulation and encounter with a seemingly "taboo" topic opened a window into the human condition—why the hell a drug-fueled, pleasure seeking, self-centered Valley boy would all of a sudden "mature" into a wannabe intellectual contemplating the mysteries of death and the human condition is a question that still boggles my mind, but also gives me deep pleasure as I reflect back.

The first half of my college career was directionless and half-hearted; the second half was a complete 180-degree turnaround from that. Determined and driven, I began to sit in the front of my classes, got to know my professors, and settled into a routine that brought a completely different level of fulfillment to my existence. And strangely, death was at the heart of this fulfillment. I finished with a BA in Psychology, though by the end I grew increasingly suspicious about my own aspirations to be a therapist and ability to carry the emotional weight of all those clients. I also grew increasingly cynical of the whole enterprise and gradually realized that most Psychology majors are nuts.

But in the last couple of years of college, I began to take courses in Religious Studies, a scholarly world I had never heard of, nor ever imagined I would be interested in, until those few semesters at California State University, Northridge. In courses on the films of Ingmar Bergman, existential thought, Christian theology, comparative religion, psychology of religion, and other fascinating topics, a part of my personality I never knew existed came to the surface, and I found myself loving school, listening closely to my professors, speaking up in class, getting the feel for scholarly arguments and styles, and enjoying greatly being around and in conversation with smart people who like to think.

The world of Religious Studies was also perfectly suited for my own peculiar intellectual fixations on death, so as I neared the end of my undergraduate studies my life as a student pretty much revolved around death, psychology, and religion. Fortunately, as I finished the degree, I also had another stark and dramatic realization that made an impact on the direction of my life: I realized I did not want to work like most of my friends—and the rest of the adult world—did after the college years, so began to see that the only viable path ahead for me was obvious: more school, which meant applying to graduate programs.

If the beginning of my undergraduate college years had a youthful and directionless vibe to them, by the end it had a more mature and focused vibe, though without question it was still driven by pleasure, play, and personal fulfillment, though now experienced quite differently in my more cerebrally focused life. So without really thinking about planning for the future, or building toward a particular career, I went ahead with utter selfishness and finagled a way for me to remain in the comforting, satisfying, and oh-so-stimulating life of higher education.

Fortunately, out of the six applications I sent in for graduate studies, with three in Psychology programs and three in Religion programs, I was accepted to a total of three. All of my applications highlighted the area of graduate study I wished to pursue so I felt certain each of the programs could guide me through doctoral studies and dissertation writing. It was a hugely important decision, obviously, so I decided to visit the three schools.

First, I went to visit Pittsburgh's Duquesne University and met with people associated with the existentialist and humanistic oriented

13

program in the Department of Psychology in late fall of 1985. The cold concrete buildings and the grey, cloudy skies were alluring at the time, though I still wasn't sure psychology would be the most fulfilling academic pursuit. Then, I went to Chicago to see the Divinity School at the University of Chicago, in winter. It was snowing madly, it seemed like there were hundreds of candidates visiting, and we were treated like cattle as I remember it. But great buildings.

Finally, I drove up the coast in early spring to the University of California, Santa Barbara, which is located on the beach, with a beautiful coastline, bike lanes, and year-round incredible weather. What I didn't know at the time, and didn't really matter since I knew where I would be going to pursue my doctorate as soon as I stepped foot on the campus, is that the Religious Studies program there was one of the best in the world, and luckily for me, it was peaking during my years there from 1986 through 1994.

The very first event of the academic year, my first as a graduate student in the Department of Religious Studies at UCSB, provided me with a reassuring signal that this was indeed the right path. In the fall of 1986, at the department's annual beginning of the year potluck celebration, all the faculty, office staff, and students gathered in a large campus reception room on the cliffs of Goleta overlooking the ocean. We had lots of food and drinks available as the sun was setting that evening, with lots of socializing and mingling inside and out. As the fifty or so of us all sat down at tables set up in a big circle, the chair of the department, at that time Phil Hammond, brought everyone together and initiated what was to become a very familiar, standard academic practice in my life: going around the room and having each person give their name and their areas of interest.

I was on Phil's right, and he started the ritual on his left side. While these can be completely time consuming and all too frequently used as opportunities for self-aggrandizement and blowing lots of hot air, this round-robin was quite captivating to me. Second-temple Judaism, Buddhist philosophy, medieval Islam, sociology of religion, history of religions, religion and philosophy, and so many other traditions and approaches in the study of religion that people noted—it felt like my head was going to explode, but in a good way. I was loving it, and the wine and effervescence in the room made the atmosphere that much more enjoyable and community building.

It soon occurred to me that I would be the last one to speak, and that this festival of introductions was dragging on a bit even with all the fascinating bits of information about my new colleagues and friends. It struck me that I only had one choice as the exercise started winding down to my turn, a mantra that I have said to myself throughout my professional career: "less is more."

When it came my turn to introduce myself, I stood up like everyone else had done, saw that I had their attention, and said: "My name is Gary Laderman, and I'm interested in death." When I finished and it was clear to everyone that that was all I was going to say, there was a brief moment of silence, and then the whole room burst out laughing and clapping. I had no idea what the hell it was all about but soon realized that I was a man in black—long and full black hair (no grey yet), black tee-shirt, black jeans, black sport coat—and death my calling card. With the intros over, and people free to mill about the room, a number of folks came over to learn more about what exactly I was up to in Religious Studies. But it felt like the room was mine, and I knew I was on to something.

2.

Death Studies Us

I spent the first year of graduate school trying to figure out what I was supposed to be doing in graduate school. This wasn't a science program, so no labs, mad experiments, or demanding professors; nor was it a social science program, immediately plowing over students with hard data, soulless analysis, and rigid structures of assessment. I was starting a Religious Studies graduate program, for God's sake, on the beach, with Isla Vista, a world-famous party college town for undergrads, next door, with pretty consistent 70-degree weather, and with a pervasive California "find your own way" scholarly vibe.

At first glance, this might not seem to be the ideal environment to be thinking studiously, or maybe more appropriately, I will admit, obsessively, about death. Santa Barbara is brimming with life, beauty, youth, intimations of eternal bliss. But the University of California, Santa Barbara, a little island paradise in my memory, was in fact ideally suited for reflections on mortality, decomposing corpses, and funerals.

It took me about a year to get my bearings, and start to understand the strange, and utterly bizarre, world of academia better. Required graduate seminars in the history of theory and method in the study of religion provided me with key landmarks in my little part of the world—Rudolph

17

Otto's idea of the holy; Émile Durkheim's elementary forms of religious life; Mary Douglas on purity and pollution; Charles Long on significations and critiques in the field; Clifford Geertz on the cockfight; and other mind-blowing classics. Taking seminars outside of my comfort zone, on Buddhist philosophy or Augustine, European Art History or the Native Americas expanded my knowledge of "religion" but also deepened a more general sense that death was at the core of it all.

That first year in graduate school had a big impact, though in more general terms broadening my knowledge base at the time, and helped confirm two of my newfound life commitments then: I loved the life of the mind, and I never wanted to work 9 to 5 like most of my friends were doing. Reading all day, or all night as the case may be; no deep and demanding structures; freedom to think and pursue ideas by oneself or even better with others about life and existence; being surrounded by lots of smart and engaging people interested in "religion" in all of its various forms, traditions, expressions, and dimensions—the first year was an introduction to a surreal, isolated, insulated, and wonderful world.

Then, everything changed. Intellectually, that is. I met the faculty member who would become my mentor, advisor, and long-time friend, Richard Hecht. Hecht was a historian of religions whose area of expertise was ancient and modern Judaism, which were and remain to this day very far afield from my own interests. At the time, during my first year in grad school, my focus remained on the psychology of religion and death, so our paths didn't really cross. But after he got wind and learned more about my questions and pursuits, he called and asked if we could meet in the fall of 1987. I told him I'd be happy to meet, and that I could come over to his office. I was a little surprised when he said no, not there, and that he preferred I meet him at the Santa Barbara Mission, about 10 miles south of the university in the city of Santa Barbara, on the following Saturday. Odd, I thought, but I had not been there and had no reason to say no, so why not?

I met him early at the mission, and as we started walking through the historic church it crossed my mind that perhaps this wasn't the best idea, since most churches, temples, mosques, and other houses of worship make me extremely antsy and uncomfortable. But we quickly exited through a doorway from the interior of the church space to the exterior of an enclosed garden-like area that was obviously the church cemetery, though a bit different and unfamiliar to me since at that time I had only set foot in Jewish and Protestant cemeteries, not Catholic ones. It was truly gorgeous in its own way, and so peaceful.

I knew immediately as soon as we sat down on a bench in the cemetery, before we started conversing for the next couple of hours, that Richard was my man, and that something in my graduate school life was about to change.

His first request of me was simple: "Tell me what you see." I looked around and started describing the scene, which included various aspects of the space, like the vegetation, cemetery walls, crypts and family vaults, statuary, large and small crosses, skull and crossbones above the doorway leading into the church, and so on. A litany of sights, details, symbols, objects that grew more and more fascinating as I tried to impress him, and really "see" what was in that cemetery space.

Then Richard started talking, and to cut to the chase, by the end of our subsequent conversation my entire scholarly perspective on death was reoriented. Psychological and more philosophical questions about death were no longer central, or even relevant, to my intellectual path. Instead, walking out of the cemetery and back to my car, I realized that my central questions about death in graduate school would be historical, and the primary focus of my studies, the corpse.

That, I realize, is quite a dramatic, and quite frankly, macabre reorientation to take place in the space of a Saturday morning at the mission, but it is the unvarnished truth, and I remember that morning as vividly as I remember writing that last sentence. During our conversation we talked mostly about what I didn't see: a mission cemetery that was rooted in a complex religious, cultural, political history of Catholic colonization; in systems of oppression and class; in multiple and diverse forms of Christian theology; and in the unmarked graves of native Chumash Indians, whose deaths brought life, in some ways, to the material power of the mission and the work of Christianity. What became crystal clear to me, and a compelling, driving intellectual force in my scholarly life from that day, was that the dead are with us and do speak to us, the living, about the never-ending human striving for meaning, purpose, knowledge, power, and perhaps most poignantly, transcendence over death.

Looking back at that pivotal cemetery meeting, I see it now as more of an initiation than simply a conversation with my new advisor. Although I would never claim this at the time, after that visit I became a scholar, or at least driven by newfound scholarly energy that I did not know I had, and that sustained me for the next eight or so years as a doctoral student. It was obvious to me at the time, however, that I was on a different path than most of the people I knew in my mid-twenties, a path that didn't entail "work," or the chance of financial success, or much structure at all. It felt so right, and the passion for learning that emerged in my undergrad years really took over in these years.

Except for that one time I started interning at a Los Angeles music company where Dave Orleans, one of my close friends worked, and almost dropped out of grad school. I don't want to leave the impression that graduate school is all light and joy, and will admit to periods of serious doubt, uncertainty, and questioning. It was a brief flirtation with what seemed to be a more glamorous and potentially prosperous path only ninety miles south, in the alluring bastion of entertainment and celebrity. I lasted about two months before returning full force to the scholarly life, but greatly valued and learned from this chance to step out into the real world. My friend, on the other hand, went on to become a major player in music distribution and the new digital music industry.

I did finish a master's thesis by the end of my second year, on death in Pre-Raphaelite Art, a nineteenth-century British movement of artists dedicated to more romantic, religious, and moralistic aesthetics than those taught at the Royal Academy of Art. By my third year in grad school, however, my studies had a three-pronged orientation: death, American history, and cultural studies in religion. The faculty I worked with in these areas all encouraged a broader view of religion and religious life, one that understood that in fact religion and culture are closely intertwined, sometimes bleed into each other and can be confused and confusing, but together generate wildly divergent, often surprising, forms of religious expression and sacred values. In this stimulating, open-minded but humanely rigorous scholarly environment, I could see that the data available for cultural analysis was limitless, and in some cases would allow me to blur the boundaries between my own personal enjoyments and academic research.

One of the most memorable, and enjoyable, seminar research papers I wrote focused on the theme of death and loss in one of my favorite songs at the time, Bruce Springsteen's "Reason to Believe." The song hit all of my intellectual buttons: death, Americana, popular culture, religious life, all mixed together in Springsteen's lyrical imagery that highlight experiences of loss—a man with his dead dog, a woman whose man walks out on her, the death of an old man, and a groom left at the altar.

Not very uplifting, right? All of this sadness, as the title suggests, does not lead to despair, depression, or dejection, but the exact opposite. Each verse ends with the words "people find some reason to believe." Hope wins in the face of death, lost love, solitude in this little ditty that closes out the album *Nebraska*, a stark, powerful, mostly despairing meditation on America's heartland in the early 1980s.

The more grad seminars I took, the more convinced I became that thinking about death had its advantages, and that in this particular scholarly context, I would find a topic that could ground my dissertation project, possibly lead to a first book, and perhaps even help get me some kind of academic job. What better setting to learn about death in all its manifestations and forms than in a doctoral program in religion? Every single class offered in the program could potentially be relevant for a death education, so it seemed like heaven to me.

By the time I reached the two critical moments in the pro-gram — comprehensive exams and dissertation proposal, moments of high anxiety, devastating stress, and near-complete mental breakdown, for many of us at least — the research and studies I had done thus far led me to two undeniable, incredibly intriguing and, fortunately for me at the time, remarkably understudied social realities in America.

One of the most challenging, potentially maddening, tasks for any-one working on their PhD is to say something no one else has said, ideally, or say what others have said in a new way, as is the case for most Humanities doctoral students. For me, as I buried myself in the liter-ature on death in America, I kept coming upon a sentence, or maybe a paragraph, in just about every study on the topic, that alluded to the most transformational moment in the history of death in America. But no scholar attempted to really unpack and dig deeper to tell the longer story about that moment.

The moment? The Civil War of course. Its impact on American atti-tudes toward death and on how Americans handled corpses would be-come the subject of my dissertation research and writing for the next three years of my life and, indeed, my very lifeblood.

The other social reality about death in America that was abundant-ly evident and overly researched in the literature seemed completely and entirely wrong to me, and this too began to drive (and still drives, obviously) my scholarly pursuits on the topic. Basically, the common perspective is that America is a death-denying culture, a society where death is taboo, particularly in the modern era, beginning roughly at the turn of the twentieth century. My research in the field, as well as growing research pursuits outside of America in anthropological cross-cultural studies on death, led me to the opposite conclusion: America is obsessed with death and in fact Americans can't stop thinking about it. Like all human cultures.

I did pass those comprehensive exams, in American history, religion and culture, the cultural history of religions, and the history of death; I also successfully defended my dissertation proposal, which centered on the question above: what impact did the Civil War have on attitudes toward death in America? At that point I entered the "no man's land" known as being ABD—"all but dissertation"—in a truly liminal state where one is no longer a student, but not yet a Doctor (of Philosophy). 1989 to 1994, probably one of the best stretches in my life.

Luckily, I was driven by a strong intellectual curiosity that even in this wonderfully liberating liminality was focused and disciplined. I also kind of liked pretending to be a scholar, and I loved telling people what I was doing: full-time graduate student in Religious Studies doing research for a dissertation on death in America (quite likely back in the day, dressed in black). You might think that would be a conversation stopper, but you would be wrong. From then to now, it seems to strike a chord and gets people talking about funerals they have attended, or memories of a near-death experience, or what a priest once said about eternity, and so on.

During those years my life became my dissertation, and my dissertation, my life—don't get me wrong, I still had many friends, enjoyed life's simple pleasures, and lived with my best friend and lover. Still, I had death on the brain, and most of the time, during weekends, early mornings, afternoons, evenings, I was either reading, researching, or thinking about the death project. I also had Richard advising me, and his first piece of advice after I became ABD was, in a word, "epic."

He thought I needed to get away from America, bone up on my critical theory and cultural studies, and get even more immersed in the

23

larger historiographical literature on the study death. What better place to do all this, he said, than in Paris, France. I followed his advice, learned French (reading pretty well, speaking, not so great), applied to and got in to the Education Abroad Program associated with the University of California. Before I knew it, in August 1989, I was sitting at the grave of Jim Morrison in Père Lachaise and reading Roland Barthes's *Camera Lucida*—a book about death and photography, and about the death of the author's mother.

My time in Paris, and France more widely, was devoted to mortuary site visits, for sure, including many hours of meandering research in Père Lachaise and other famous Parisian cemetery tourist destinations, as well as in catacombs, churchyards, and American military cemeteries. While my eyes were feasting on the scenery, and my stomach luxuriating in the food, my mind consumed big ideas and intricate theories in the books I was reading, the classes I was taking, and the people I was meeting. The French, too, are obsessed with death, but they are much more self-aware and intellectually engaged with it than Americans, who just live with and are driven by their deathly obsessions, and don't really want to think about why they think so much about the topic.

There is no doubt in my mind that during the year my close encounters with three pivotal French intellectuals gave me the necessary tools to conceptually refine and then ultimately execute the writing of the dissertation. Two of them were dead, so my familiarity with their work was based entirely on reading the French texts of each thinker, often in the tiny chambre de bonne, or maid's quarters on the top floor of the seven-story apartment building where I lived on the outskirts of Paris. The other one was kind enough to engage with me in an independent, one-on-one study, which took place in his office at the Sorbonne every couple of weeks or so.

Philippe Ariès is perhaps the most well-known historian of death (I know, there aren't many). His life spanned much of the twentieth century, and his innovative historical studies on various intriguing topics like childhood and everyday life, gave him an international reputation beyond France. His magnus opus on death is *The Hour of Our Death*, a near 800-page tome on the history of attitudes toward death in Western and primarily Christian cultures, and based on lectures he gave at Johns Hopkins University in 1956.

Ariès's historical explorations of changing attitudes, and his identification of five dominant types in this history, provided a model of analysis and mode of cultural interpretation that I continue to use to this day in my death and dying classes. The five attitudes Ariès describes include: "tamed death" which is a deep-rooted and longstanding view in western cultural history that has all but vanished in the modern world and is accepting of death, familiar with it, and helps a community calmly prepare for the end; "one's own death," which shifts the focus to the individual encounter with death and a growing concern about the ultimate fate of the individual soul, emerges early in the Christian era and continues to inform some views to this day; the most interesting of the bunch, "remote and imminent death," in which a strange mixture of eroticism, violence, and ambivalence associated with death is culturally heightened in the fifteenth through eighteenth centuries (think the Marquis de Sade, if you dare); "thy death," an attitude that in a sense domesticates and beautifies death and is obviously located squarely in the Romantic era of the nineteenth century; and finally, the dominant cultural attitude of Ariès's contemporary world from the first half of the twentieth century, and a view many think still holds to this day, "forbidden death." Those last two attitudes specifically connect to American trends and would become integral to my own thinking about the impact of the Civil War on American attitudes.

In some ways diametrically opposed to Ariès is Michel Vovelle, a French historian who wrote primarily on the French Revolution and the history of death. While Ariès was clearly politically and religiously conservative, Vovelle was a leftist through and through whose Marx-ist-tinged historical analyses are nuanced, dense, and complicated. I met periodically with Vovelle during my year in Paris, and he tolerated my poorly spoken French when we weren't just talking in English in his office. It was intimidating to take the metro to one of the more famous universities in the world and walk through those halls and by busts of famous thinkers, but utterly enjoyable because of his genuine enthusi-asm for historical questions and apparent interest in my questions and research pursuits.

Vovelle also produced a magnus opus, but it didn't have nicely, neatly framed attitudes to drive the historical narrative like Ariès. *La mort et l'Occident de 1300 à nos jours* is a grand Marxist take on death in west-ern culture, full of sterling and careful analyses of class differences and religious excesses, popular expressions and elite philosophies over sev-eral centuries. But truly his masterpiece is a briefer, more focused ex-amination of wills in eighteenth century Provence, France, *Piété baroque et déchristianisation en Provence au XVIIIe siècle*. Our conversations pur-sued his work, and my research plans, and made an impression on my thinking about methodology in historical studies, and the relationships between Christianity, power, and death in western cultures.

In one of our final conversations I asked him what he thought about the other dead French intellectual whose books I was devouring during my time in Paris. When I mentioned the name, Michel Foucault, to Vovelle he looked me squarely in the eyes and warned me about being seduced by "le diable." To this day I'm not sure if he was playing with me or genuinely warning me about the dangers of Foucault the Devil. We just left it at that and continued to discuss my dissertation proj-ect. I didn't bring Foucault up again with Vovelle, but continued to read through his devilish writings, including *The Order of Things*, *Madness and Civilization*, and *Discipline and Punish*.

The one book of Foucault's, however, that hit me like a ton of bricks was *The Birth of the Clinic*, first published in 1963. In short, it gave me a brilliant example of how to make the corpse work as the center of a historical narrative and cultural analysis. For Foucault, the emerging medical practices and reformulation of medical knowledge in eighteenth-century France were tied to the new space of the "clinic" and new ways of perceiving the corpse. Rather than simply a natural outgrowth of great advances in medicine up to that point, Foucault claims an "epistemic shift" or rupture in the structure of medical knowledge took place, and with it new ways to imagine the values of the dead body surfaced and took hold, values not determined by the church or clergy purportedly for the purposes of saving souls, but by the expanding scientific and medical authorities who were primarily interested in and motivated by dissections and autopsies purportedly for the purposes of improving health.

The journalistic motto, "follow the money," has yielded a great many newsworthy scoops in politics. The research motto that began to fuel my dissertation investigative fires after reading Foucault's book was, "follow the corpse." Morbid? Yes. But for anyone who studies religion, or even thinks about religion, the corpse is a no-brainer data point, since everyone knows that religious life comes to life in the face of this peculiar, hard-to-define, material object remaining at death. Thanks to Foucault, I began to see the revelatory cultural value of studying the corpse, front and center, and also realized how little scholarly attention had been directed to the dead body in American religious history.

That year in France set up the conceptual themes and contours of the project, and when I returned to the California coast in the summer of 1990, the next three years of my non-working but always working life was devoted to original research, which meant digging through primary sources and figuring out an original story they tell about how the past bears on the present; and then beginning the truly grueling, back breaking, mind-boggling process of writing a god damn book (a dissertation is pretty close to the same thing, if one is lucky), something I never would have imagined doing in my wildest dreams as a younger man. France and its scholarly traditions and approaches to history provided me with the intellectual tools to think differently about the corpse and death. Now it was up to me to find the content, the meat, in answer to a specific historical question: how did the Civil War impact American attitudes toward death?

Exploring answers to that question on my own as a research scholar was just as stimulating and fulfilling as my year in France as a student learning critical theories and histories. But instead of hallowed halls of higher education in western Europe and stuffy fashionable intellectuals in the cafés of Paris, my research led me to the rural highways and back-roads of New England and musty archives in collections with warm and helpful librarians. Thanks to the always sage advice of my dissertation committee, I limited my historical focus to the North, and bracketed the timeframe with the deaths of two US Presidents: George Washington's death in 1799, and Abraham Lincoln's death in 1865.

With clear boundaries set for the project, I embarked on various re-search trips from UCSB to locations throughout the northeast, some-times alone and sometimes with my partner Liz, and often staying with friends and relatives here and there. In all candor, I have to admit that this research work was a blast and incredibly easy for one very simple reason: death was everywhere in the nineteenth century—everyone was talking about it, writing about it, thinking about it, encountering it, struggling against it, embracing it, and basically finding ways to live with it. The historical and material evidence of this prevalence and articulated preoccupation is, in a word, magnificent, which made primary sources both readily and easily available, and utterly fascinating.

Death, it seemed to me, was on everyone's mind back then. Its pres-ence and aftereffects were tangible, and often quite devastating, in the words of many Americans who kept diaries and wrote letters to convey their thoughts, experiences, and comments about the everyday realities of death in their lives. Popular cultures of the time, mainly limited to forms of popular literature, gave these realities new life—sometimes romanticized, but also represented grimly, graphically, and violently—for nineteenth-century American readers. Politicians and Christian leaders brought the spirits of the dead, and fears about death, to public consciousness as well, in the case of the former to tighten the bonds of national identity, in the case of the latter to save souls for Christ. Cemeteries, too, spoke volumes about the presence of death and how people thought about it, so research visits that consisted of walking through both rural and urban nineteenth century sites were essential and illuminating.

The corpse was an integral and visible part of this landscape, and so played a familiar role in the scenery of these everyday realities in the writings, imagination, and rhetoric of the time and culture. The data I began to accumulate and record was robust, daunting almost, but also rife with interpretive possibilities for understanding how religious cultures change through a thorough grounding in an era's attitudes toward death. Antebellum America proved to be a culturally rich and expressive era, with death and the dead body unavoidable, always accessible, and undeniably central in the primary sources for white, primarily Christian, northern religious cultures of the time.

The impact of the carnage from the Civil War left its mark in the archives too, as well as in just about every facet of American society during and after the conflict. An awful, brutal, tragic period in the lives of many Americans, for sure; but also, for me, a happy treasure trove of data and sources to study and better understand the impact of death during this war on American attitudes, both during the war itself and how it prefigured dramatic changes in American views during the twentieth century.

As a grad student who was beginning to think of himself as a budding historian, I was striking primary data gold because the topics of my investigation—death, attitudes toward death, the treatment of the dead — were ubiquitous in historical records, archives, media and literature, and so on, and always, in some way, related to weighty and meaningful religious sensibilities that were diverse and changing.

It would be inaccurate, and unfair, to characterize my time as a young and enthusiastic researcher running free in cemeteries and libraries in simplistic and idyllic terms. It did take a toll and made its own impact on me, in my pocketbook, but also more seriously and impressively in my soul. I am not sure how to put it without sounding trite if not silly, but all of the research digging, reading, reflecting, and so on definitely put me in touch with the dead. Literally, just in the way I spent time in cemeteries littered with the dead and their grave markers, and handled letters and diaries that included intimate reflections and expressed sentiments for one's own eyes or the eyes of others; but also, on another, less literal and material level I felt the presence of the dead.

Reading through the letters of long-dead Civil War soldiers, for example, was both chilling and energizing. The immediacy of war, and keen awareness of death captured in the words of so many soldiers' letters I held in my own hands, brought me both existentially and imaginatively into a unique and powerful relationship with the dead — not as if they were "speaking" to me, but more like they were present with me, in those letters and in the imagined lives that took shape as I read through various files.

One ghost from those research days continues to live with me even as the decades pass and I struggle to live with the more recent ghosts I think about so often now. This individual came to life in death for me at the Huntington Library, where I was lucky enough to be researching Civil War archives in a beautiful locale and gardens, and came across a particular file with a series of letters inside. Nothing too profound or elaborate in the letters from this northern solider sent home to his wife, just descriptions of the new normal conditions of life, and death, during wartime.

I can't remember how many letters were in the file but there were more than a few and as I flipped each letter with my latex gloved hand, and took notes that would bring life to my nascent professional career, an impossible, and impossibly strange bond formed between this soldier and myself. Perhaps similar to the wife in some sense, I began reading each letter with a mixture of sadness and despair about the circumstances surrounding this young man, and gleeful anticipation for what kernels of hope and inspiration I might get out of these fragile pages scrawled with words from an era so long ago.

The final document in the file took me by surprise. I wasn't ready for it even though in retrospect, I often think that I should have known where this life in letters would end. The last letter in the file was from the government, letting the recipient know that her loved one had died in battle. It was an abrupt end to an archival dalliance with a long dead American who was one of the hundreds of thousands killed during that internal conflict and whose lives are meaningless now, except for those who continue to think about and imagine some kind of connection with them.

I took a few years but finally, by 1993, my dissertation was completed, defended, and approved, and it was finally time to transition to the next phase of life, if I could find a position somewhere. Soon after I began applying across the country to any teaching job that looked reasonably close to what my training and education could offer, I said something to Liz that no doubt sealed our fate. I said "I'll take any job, as long as it's not in the South." My first three on-campus interviews were with Rice University, in Houston, Texas; Duke University in North Carolina; and Emory University, in Atlanta, Georgia. In the fall of 1994, my wife and I moved from Santa Barbara to Atlanta, where I started my first and only job.

3.

Becoming a Death Expert

During my on-campus interview at Emory University for the job in the Department of Religion, two interactions led me to believe I would get what was I soon realized, a plum job. First, for my public presentation I focused on the end point of my dissertation—the death, embalming, and funeral journey of Abraham Lincoln. It really was some of the best material, and so compelling as a pivot point between the old ways of death and the new, modern way of death. I decided to go no holds barred, and get as graphic, and detailed, and unsparing as possible in my descriptions of the treatment and fate of Lincoln's dead body after the assassination and before the final interment.

After the presentation, I was approached by one of the more eminent historians of American religion, Brooks Holifield, a faculty member at the Candler School of Theology at Emory. He liked the argument and seemed to be genuinely enthused and intrigued by the emphasis on the sacred, rather than theology, when exploring the religious meanings, values, and practices associated with Lincoln's corpse in 1865. This southern Californian had something of a change of heart in that one interaction with a gracious and superstar scholar born and raised in the South, and teaching at a southern theology school to boot. Many perceptions and misconceptions about intellectual life in the South were overcome in the fifteen minutes or so after my talk, and I felt warmly welcomed and strangely at home in the diverse and smart religion community at Emory.

The second interaction occurred over a one-on-one dinner with Eugene Bianchi, a former Jesuit originally from northern California with publications covering a range of topics, including theology, ecology, and aging. The dinner itself was pleasant and lively, but one moment in the conversation stands out and, looking back, opened a door in my professional trajectory that has brought me some of my most fulfilling professorial experiences.

We were talking about the course he had been teaching at Emory for twenty years at that point in 1993, "Death and Dying," when I began to wonder, and worry, about whether he saw me as someone trying to hone in on his turf, that perhaps he felt threatened by my intellectual and pedagogical interests. This, by the way, is common in academia world, where insecurities, paranoias, and subterfuge are a way of life, especially as one navigates their way through tenure. But in this case, as we were talking and my anxieties lessened with some wine and food, he came out and said bluntly: "I'll be glad to turn this class over to you when you're hired." Yes, he spoke as if I had already been offered the job, but even more memorable was the genuine sentiment behind the offer, and the sense of excitement about what I might do with the course given my training and intellectual proclivities.

In one of the more unusual, and I believe highly rare, moments in higher education, I was offered the job by the Chairperson at the time, Paul Courtright, on the spot, before I even left the campus after my interview.

I hit the ground running my first semester teaching and offered Bianchi's old course, now mine, "Death and Dying," which has become a staple in my curricular offerings over twenty-five years at Emory. I don't want to say I was born to teach this course, but thinking retrospectively, I had some early seeds planted to prepare me for the class, even before graduate school. Believe it or not, both my junior high and high schools in the San Fernando Valley offered a death and dying course as an elective, and I took the course in both settings, for reasons I can't recall, but likely having something to do with enhancing my popularity with my peers and not content, at the time.

As an undergraduate I also had a course on the topic that made more of an impact because of its attempt at breadth, thinking across cultures and about some of the deeper questions that come with reflecting on death. It was also taught by a Japanese Buddhist, which added a completely new wrinkle to my own reflections at the time, but also alerted me to the supreme value of comparative, cross cultural thinking on the topic for young adults like me, who start to think about death at that age in new ways.

"Death and Dying" is a favorite of mine, for sure, but the class also seems to have grown into a favorite for undergrads over the years as well—in that first semester there were eight or so students enrolled; now when I teach it the course can easily enroll 300. In all honesty, I think I hit upon a winning pedagogical formula for the syllabus and the class experience, a logic and structure that I also later applied to another course that seems to have struck a chord with students, "Religion and Sexuality."

The formula is simple. To start at the endpoint, a top priority in the class is to get students to see their world differently by the end of the term, and especially how they see and understand religion, and the place of death in contemporary America. The course unfolds in three stages: First, we do a brief and cursory overview of death in a variety of cultural settings, except Christian. So the idea is to think comparatively and openly about death in Buddhist or Islamic or Native American or

African or Jewish cultures, focusing on obvious questions like, what is done with the corpse, or how is the afterlife understood, or why do the living rely on ritual activity in the face of death? This is set up purposely to disorient students, and get them to encounter what are often foreign, and for them incredibly diverse, attitudes about such questions.

The second stage of the course moves to a close historical analysis of death in the history of Christianity, something many students think they are familiar with, but as we explore various Christian cultural topics, like the cult of saints, the invention of purgatory, and the centrality of original sin for understanding bodily corruption, they soon realize how the study of death brings strange but insightful perspectives into what is for many of them their own particular tradition.

With this social history of Christianity, or better, Christianities in the west, as the ground beneath their feet, so to speak, we move to the third stage in the class, a historical and thematic exploration of death in America. This is a blast for me and for them for a number of reasons. On the one hand, the students get to learn about all kinds of unusual and wonderful elements from American religious history—yes of course, the Puritans are included, but also spiritualism, grave robbing, African-derived religious practices, as well as my own unique take on the evolution and innovations in American funeral traditions.

On the other hand, I try to keep it real, and relevant to their worlds and experiences, so we start every session of the semester with something we all relate too: music. I ask them to choose death-related songs and send them to me, the class DJ—though I will certainly throw in some of my favorites, like George Harrison's "The Art of Dying," or Wilco's "On and On and On," or Uncle Tupelo's "No Depression" or Bone Thugs N Harmony, "Crossroads."

At first when I bring this exercise up at the beginning of the semester, they wonder about my sanity, but by the end of the term we are all amazed at the ubiquity of the topic in their playlists. Early in my teaching, I reserved two full sessions for listening to music and discussing the songs, but by the end of those classes we all were so emotionally wiped out—it was simply too intense—that I had to change the rhythm of the exercise. Just for good medicine, I also like to arrange for Emory-associated musicians to perform and play death-themed classical pieces for the students, and me.

Another enjoyable death course exercise that keeps the students on their toes are the site visits. Yes, in classes with 5 or 250 students enrolled, I make sure they don't just think, and read, and listen to me about death, but that they see it, up close and personal, firsthand. We have visited local funeral homes, preferably those with crematoria, and always go to the historic Oakland Cemetery, Atlanta's own version of a "rural" cemetery that became so popular in the mid-nineteenth century, and includes graves that are now popular tourist sites—for the legendary golfer Bobby Jones, the author of *Gone with the Wind*, Margaret Mitchell, or former mayor Maynard Jackson, to name a few.

The city of Atlanta has a great deal to offer a class on death and dying, but so does Emory University, which is ideally and surprisingly suited for my own macabre sensibilities and pedagogic choices. First, I find it a strange coincidence that I ended up at a university with a skeleton as a mascot. It's true. Dooley is the beloved and mysterious "spirit of Emory," rooted deep in the schools past but alive today, most visibly during Dooley week when a student, dressed as a skeleton, representing a spirit, makes surprise visits in various college classes. The spirit has come to my class, many times.

Additionally, the superb Michael C. Carlos museum includes an excellent collection of ancient Egyptian mummies and is usually across the quad from where the course is offered. Instead of a lecture on death in ancient Egypt, I send them to the museum and then we discuss what they "learned" about death in that cultural context—ancient Egypt but also the context of a modern museum. Finally, the coup de grace and one of my favorite places to bring them is a highly disturbing and uncomfortable space, for many. I warn them that some students have felt faint, others have regretted going, and others entered the space but immediately left. On the other hand, I tease, some were transformed, others transfixed, and still others totally bored by the visit. All these visits are voluntary, not required, so I encourage those who aren't sure, not to go. This particularly sacred site (at least in my book): the morgue at Emory hospital, which is conveniently located over the cafeteria and an easy walk across the quad.

In other words, you could say I spend the entire semester getting 18 to 22-year-olds to think about death, though my twist is that we think together about death with a shared focus on a peculiar though revelatory and repugnant object at the center of the story, the corpse. The dead body is front and center from the get-go for students, in the syllabus and in much of the theoretical and, on my good days, comedic materials I present in the first few sessions. But there's more to it than blood and bones, and we certainly run through a gamut of topics — though, to be honest, the two subjects I tended to superficially gloss over in class because of their emotional volatility were end-of-life care and suicide. That has changed in recent years.

I have to admit to having mixed feelings about my pedagogic mission in this class since I know, am absolutely certain, the course can make an impact on these young, young adults, not just in terms of intellectual knowledge, growing through exposure to new cultural practices and histories, but existentially, in terms of their sense of self, meaning, purpose, and relation to others in this fairly stark, though educationally safe, confrontation with mortality. I'm not a parent, or a preacher, or a grief counselor, or a funeral director for them. The class clearly opens up a space for thinking together about one of the most critical, meaningful, impressive, unavoidable experiences for any human. My sense is that it is valuable, especially for this age group.

But on the other hand, this might sound over the top, but I also worry it does in some ways hasten and alter the transition, to keep the musical motif going, from "songs of innocence" to "songs of experience." In other words, to be more direct, I feel some guilt in bringing all this to the forefront—it's not like economics, or political science, or English, or other courses in their so-called "liberal arts" education. It strikes deep, whether they're in the class because someone they know has died, are already morbidly interested in the topic, or hear that I'm an easy grader, and it gets uncomfortable if not disorienting to some students.

For myself, in those first few years at Emory, untenured and utterly naive, I had big plans to move my research trajectory on to another path, beyond death. My dissertation was turned into a book, *The Sacred Remains: American Attitudes Toward Death, 1799-1883*, and published by Yale University Press two years after I started, in 1996, when my first son, Graham, was born too. As a thirty-something married adult, now with my first child and a second, Miles, born a couple years later, I thought I could teach the death class, but the next book would be on a different, more life-affirming topic, like religion and film, or religion and healing. My plan, in other words, was to stop thinking so much about death in this new stage of life.

Another epic fail.

Fortunately, the publication of my first book and my other professional commitments and engagements were deemed worthy enough by my peers to allow me to enter the golden realm of tenured professors after six years, moving from assistant professor to associate professor, and even further from the real world now that I had a job for life. The name of the game, at least professionally in the game of academia at this middle stage of life, was getting promoted from associate professor to full

39

professor. And that depended on a second book. I try to be something of a go-getter, so that second book became an urgent matter and a topic that I thought and thought and thought about. The truth is, as alluded to earlier, I tried, I really tried, to move on from death and came up with all kinds of grand ideas. But I couldn't get away from the topic and I knew—a knowledge that comes from the gut and not the brain—I had not finished with death. And so, "Death: Book Two," was born when I finally accepted what my gut kept telling me.

The first book ends with Lincoln's death and funeral journey, and what I refer to there as the "birth of the funeral industry" in the early years after the Civil War. A cultural history of the funeral home through the twentieth century had not been written, and I was compelled, inspired almost, to finish the story I started in *The Sacred Remains*. Most of my interest and training to this point had been centered in nineteenth-century religious America, so an exploration of death, and the unmistakable triumph of a funeral industry empire built on the embalmed body in the twentieth century, would bring me into uncharted but fascinating modern American religious cultures. I embraced the new project with gusto and excitement.

I knew that I was on to something when, after I settled on writing another book on death, a sequel to a fairly obscure academic book, two thoughts immediately came to mind. They captivated my intellectual curiosity because I knew without even really knowing how, they would yield great fruit for the project and propel it forward. The first relates to Jessica Mitford and is obvious to anyone who knows anything about death in the twentieth century, and became abundantly clear as I read more and more in the death literature.

Mitford's book, *The American Way of Death*, published in 1963, was a watershed book in so many incredibly important ways, and a pivot point for modern views on death and the funeral. It was a fierce and furious and fun assault on the American funeral tradition at midcentury that effectively changed American views about disposal of the dead. Basically, the thought I had, more of an informed hunch at the time, was to question whether Mitford was correct in her assessment.

The second idea that quickly surfaced in my reflections was not intellectual at all, not initially anyway. Rather than a thought drawn from books or articles I was reading, or an informed scholarly hunch about cultural patterns or collective turning points in society, this came from my core, a private, personal memory somehow formative, because so vivid and emotionally resonant, to who I am and have become. I'm not sure how old I was when I first saw the death of Bambi's mother on screen—in my case, probably like millions of other baby boomers, on the big screen in a drive-in theater with my family—but it hit me hard as a young boy, and stuck with me, at some level of consciousness, until bubbling to the surface for "Death: Book Two."

The more I thought about poor Bambi's mother and the power of the scene in my childhood, the more I began to wonder about the theme of death in other early Walt Disney films. That question, it turned out, was a goldmine and got me started on the right foot for the book project. "The Disney Way of Death," became the first article I published from the new book, and a springboard for other means of supporting the larger project, including fellowships from the American Council of Learned Societies, which allowed me take a year sabbatical, and the National Endowment for the Humanities, which allowed me to participate in a death seminar at Columbia University.

When I gave an early public presentation on death and Disney at the annual professional meeting of the American Academy of Religion, a professional gathering for religion nerds like me, it was a hit, with a large crowd, and even some newspaper coverage. The little clips from *Bambi, Snow White, Pinocchio, Fantasia,* and one of his earliest and one of my favorites, *The Skeleton Dance,* brought back memories for those in the crowd, but also hammered my points home.

41

With grants, fellowships, time, and university support, I went head-long into researching and writing what became *Rest in Peace: A Cultural History of Death and the Funeral Home in Twentieth-Century America*, which came out in 2003 with Oxford University Press and ultimately provided the stepping stone needed to move me to the next level of academic advancement, a "full" professor. Much of the textual data was similar to the materials I worked with for *The Sacred Remains*—letters, diaries, journal and newspaper publications, government documents, and so on; but with new forms of media and communications taking hold and exploding in the twentieth century, like cinema, television, radio, and much later the digital and internet revolutions, the variety and spectrum of sources related to American views on death grew exponentially, which for a historian is a good problem to have, I think.

But it is no surprise that the center holds in the sequel as it did in the first book, and the corpse and the religious cultures around it are highlighted throughout. And that meant the primary thread running through the book is the rise, triumph, and dominance of the funeral industry—and the death-centered religious culture driving that enterprise. The fact that I interviewed some real live people, mostly funeral directors, instead of reviving imagined dead lives from the past was quite different for me and offered an unusually refreshing element to the data gathering process. I spoke with funeral directors in San Antonio, Nashville, Los Angeles, Boston, and other cities whose families had been in the business for a few generations, and was given access to some of the private collections of documents and artifacts.

It was very strange, but also strangely meaningful, to sit down and talk with them and hear their stories about growing up in a funeral home, how and why they stayed in the business, and what it meant to them. The private communications I read sent from family members to the funeral homes were also profound, and all these funeral home interactions led me to question the simplicity and ad hominem nature of

Midford's long-standing and impactful arguments. Informed more with a cross-cultural, anthropological perspective on the universal but culturally variable questions surrounding disposal of the corpse, I tried to paint a more nuanced picture of American attitudes toward disposal, and how there is both continuity and change, tradition and innovation, over the course of the twentieth century.

I finished writing the book in August 2001, one month before the 9/11 attacks. For myself, after watching the planes crash into the Twin Towers and living in the intense and disorienting aftermath with the rest of the country immediately following that day, the book did not matter, and other fears and concerns took over my consciousness for some time after. But the book and its themes slowly crept back into my mind the more I was reading and learning about the carnage. In particular, the awful horror for so many grieving individuals of not having the body available for disposal seemed relevant to the overall thrust of the book and ultimately led to the writing of the epilogue, the final piece before the publication of *Rest in Peace*.

As I mentioned, the book was published in 2003 and I'm not embarrassed to admit that many in the funeral industry loved it even though it was not an explicit, full-throttled defense of the industry. Certainly, and admittedly, the book offers a more sympathetic portrait of the funeral director and attempts to contextualize both the trajectory of American funerals in larger general social and cultural currents, and the more specific confusing, confounding religious sensibilities at work when death strikes in a so-called "secularizing" modern capitalist society. While I was not a cold corpse, I did become something of a hot commodity in the funeral biz given my position as a purportedly objective "scholar" from a major university with a new book published by a prestigious press who actually talked with undertakers and did thorough historical research.

This book propelled me in some surprising but rewarding, mostly, professional directions. Perhaps not surprisingly, I was asked to give a number of public talks at funeral director association meetings. Graduate studies in Religious Studies at UC Santa Barbara did not prepare me for speaking to large and small public audiences of undertakers and a great many others affiliated with disposal of the dead in American society. But I learned to wing it, was fascinated by the living cultures animating the contemporary funeral industry, and enjoyed the attention from "real" people — not students or others within the cocoon I live in, the ivory tower.

I gave public talks all over — Grand Rapids, Michigan; Scottsdale, Arizona; Atlantic City, New Jersey; San Francisco, California; even Las Vegas, Nevada, where I heard I gave a rousing public lecture, but can't really remember much of it myself. Invitations came from International Cemetery and Funeral Association organizations, state-based Funeral Director's Associations, the Order of the Golden Rule, and a meeting for the Jewish Funeral Directors Association. Perhaps another reason I enjoyed these public interactions so much was because they were with other professionals whose lives were dedicated to thinking about death in this life, and yet who seemed to be utterly and completely comfortable living with death in mind.

Additionally, the book brought me to journalists and others in the media working on death stories, often though not always, as someone to give larger perspectives on attitudes toward death and funerals. The public interest in the topic will not die, and I became known as one of the only "specialists" out there who could speak on such topics, commenting on stories that ranged from historical overviews of American funerals; to trends in personalized memorials to the dead; to how disposal methods have changed since the 1960s; to various practices in different religious communities. The fact that I wasn't a religious leader, nor a funeral industry insider, and that I was located at Emory, of course, helped my standing as a public commenter who had clearly, if not curiously, thought a lot about death too.

In my experience, conversations with journalists writing a story were mostly pleasant and reaffirming—in the sense that we would often have very long, intense "interviews" that, I hate to say it, would turn in my mind to mini-lectures for an undergrad, with the enthusiasm and engagement in the journalist's voice sounding just as eager as a student learning a new and fascinating field of study. I would often begin the conversation with, "I only have a few minutes," and that would usually not hold true. Conversations about death and Disney, or death and the history of funerals, or comparative observations between various religious cultures, or even, and also usually without fail considering my background, about the very meaning of the word "religion," were often very lively and took us way beyond the bounds of what ultimately appeared in the article.

I wasn't simply after reaffirmation in these interactions, to be honest. I hoped and expected not only to be quoted in the story, but to have the book publicized as well, which most writers respected and ensured. Only occasionally did one, or two, or maybe three, completely drop me from the story but use ideas from the conversation. Frustrating, but not the only times "public scholarship" became a time suck, or worse.

I greatly appreciated any public interest in the book and loved sending my parents all the articles. Some stories in local newspapers even highlighted the book specifically and gave it the kind of exposure academics rarely receive. Although I wish I could say that made a difference in terms of sales, it really didn't. But something more rewarding did happen—though cash flow would have been nice too. I started to get a few letters in the mail from strangers, though most from within the funeral industry, that expressed deep appreciation for my work. In public lectures, sometimes I intuit that appreciation, sometimes I hear directly from students or someone in an audience after a lecture, but getting a letter from a stranger about your scholarship was a different kind of mind-blowing experience for me.

However, one handwritten letter stands out that came in the mail, after an article about the book, "A look at death, American-style," was published in the *Atlanta Journal Constitution* in 2005. When I read it, I was completely bowled over and it made me consider my relationship to readers in ways that I never imagined I'd have to consider. It's not every day that a letter from a death row inmate arrives, but that's what I received from an individual in a Georgia prison who read about the book, but also about the "Death and Dying" course covered in the piece.

Specifically, he was impressed with my inclusion of music in the course, and movingly wrote "There is a piece of music entitled 'Christo Regentor [sic]' done by Donald Byrd and the Black Byrds. If the time comes for me to die here, I would be greatly comforted knowing that somewhere in Georgia that piece of music was being played for me. Would you do that for me please? In either case, peace be with you." This was a segment of the public I never imagined reaching, though it would not be the last time my area of expertise brought me into the world of law and order.

Over the course of my career, and as a result of my research on death, I have served as an expert witness in a few civil lawsuits in which lawyers in the cases believed scholarly knowledge about death in America and the history of the funeral industry in particular, would serve justice. These court cases were not pleasant at all, and generally had to do with the neglect and worse of dead bodies left in the care of individuals working in some kind of mortuary capacity. Some of the cases made national headlines, with disturbingly graphic descriptions of decomposing, abused corpses in media coverage and reports of public disgust with the disturbing treatment of the dead.

Questions such as, how should the dead be treated, and who is responsible for a dignified disposal, were clearly instrumental in making legal arguments about financial compensation, if not criminal charges. Psychologists were brought in, of course; spokespeople for the funeral industry as well; forensic evidence played a particularly gruesome role in the investigations too. But calling in an academic who could really only speak to historical matters and religious sensibilities associated with the disposal of the corpse in America seemed, at least to me, a brilliant move.

I only had to take the stand in court once. The other cases required me to give a deposition and sit, in most cases, in a room with a bunch of lawyers for a long, long time. But in both settings, I have to admit that rather than disgust and ridicule, I honestly had a great deal of respect for the lawyers I met and interacted with, on both sides. On some occasions, however, I could not help wondering about the utter absurdity of some of these interactions, like being questioned by a group of over twenty lawyers in a class action suit for over three hours; or waiting nearly a whole day to take the stand—and getting paid a ridiculous amount per hour.

Being surrounded by lawyers in an unnatural setting for uncomfortable reasons is anxiety producing for sure, but the actual flow and content of these conversations were often quite exhilarating, even enjoyable at times, in a weird way. In general, these were easy interactions because I just had to stick to the script, my script, based on what I researched and then wrote about in two books and other publications about the history of American funerals. We would spend a ridiculous amount of time going over what I could not and would not comment on, such as legal statutes, or medical treatments or conditions, or operating a funeral home. But truly in many, if not most, cases the lawyers themselves became quite interested in talking about what I have learned in my studies about death.

But not always. Once in a while the nice intellectual flow would get sidetracked, and the engaging back and forth on pretty loaded topics would turn into more of a stop and go theological interrogation of my own personal views. At one point in one of the depositions I gave, the lawyer flat out asked me if I believed humans have a soul? The question came out of left field, I felt, though I often wondered when my personal views would be brought up in these intense conversations about death and what people do and expect to be done with dead bodies.

Fortunately, the lawyer who hired me stepped in and rightly objected to form. I was told I could still answer, so I told the truth, "My expertise is in history, culture, religion."

He followed up with another doozy—do I have any opinion about "whether or not a soul remains with the body after death." Again, an objection, and again, me trying to be a smart aleck: "I'm not sure I understand the question." The guy kept trying to get me to go beyond my area of expertise, and bring in my own personal views, as if they would have an impact on my scholarship or testimony. I always tried to keep my atheism under wraps in these circumstances, though referencing my Jewish upbringing seemed often to distract from too much attention on the topic of my personal religious beliefs.

But later in the deposition, when another lawyer began with follow up questions that pursued my non-scholarly perspectives on deeply religious matters, again in a court case with millions of dollars at stake dealing with profaned corpses, disgusting cemetery conditions, and grotesque forensic details, he became increasingly frustrated with my comparative obfuscations and scholarly evasions, and finally blurted out: "But I'm asking you. I'm asking you your opinion personally about whether individuals have a soul," to which I replied with a great deal of self-satisfaction, knowing it was going to blow his top, "Depends what you mean by 'soul.'"

4.

Oh Death

Death never gets old, that's for sure. I have been ambivalent at times about spending so much time professionally thinking about it, but I'm not sure I could have fallen into a better field of research, to be honest, not only because of the range and richness of all the related topics to it, but also, at least for me, because of the social rewards. Under the right circumstances, people—not just students and colleagues—love talking about it, and when they find out it's what I "do," well the floodgates open and streams of ideas and questions and stories pour out.

On one occasion I did refuse to talk about death, however. It was 1997, early in my career and not quite the confident "expert" ready to take on a roomful of lawyers. I received a call from a journalist the day after Princess Diana died from injuries in a car accident. The news of her death was a cultural jolt and, at the time, I had some reservations about propriety and respect so soon after such a terrible accident, so did not want to comment. Those kinds of reservations in the face of tragedy and collective grief were soon thrown out the window, for me and for American culture more generally, by the turn of the century. Sensational stories, talking heads, and lurid details in the right-here-right-now news cycle supersede any notions of quiet dignity, mournful meditation, or simply taking time to absorb the loss of celebrities and beloved pubic figures.

I am not sure, but I believe Diana's death occurred during a semester I was teaching Death and Dying. Indeed, it is remarkable, and quite telling that just about every year I teach the class, a celebrity dies and provides us with an opportunity to discuss the emergence and increasing repetition of an intriguing and significant social phenomenon: the religious impact following the death of famous people. My third book, *Sacred Matters* (not, I should point out, exclusively and singularly focused on mortal matters, though the final chapter is "Death") touches on this new religious reality and covers Elvis, Tupac, Valentino, and Disney to illustrate the point. In classes we have been intellectually engaged as well with a range of dead celebrities, whether the conversations turned to aging when Johnny Carson died; or new trends in funerals with Hunter S. Thompson; or accidental overdosing, with the death of Whitney Houston; or ESPN anchor Stuart Scott's battle with cancer; or the suicide of Chris Cornell. The list goes on. And on.

It does seem, more and more, that every day brings news of the death of another celebrity, or someone who was once famous for something some time ago. We are not only saturated with reminders of mortality in this morbid onslaught; in some if not many cases, people are deeply affected and experience profound sadness and grief in the aftermath. American lives are intimately tied in to the lives of celebrities — famous actors, sports heroes, reality stars, politicians, musicians, and so on — and questions about the cause and circumstances of death, funeral plans, and how to best memorialize the lost individual can be quite compelling in the minutes, hours, or days that pass until the next public death.

But on another level, on some less apparent existential plane, questions about the meaning and purpose of life, core values to live by, the true nature of individual identity, is there a life beyond this one — religious questions without doubt — can also be put into play when a screen idol, or rock star, or football legend, or political figure perishes. It is difficult thinking of a comparative set of historical circumstances, when every day large numbers of people are disturbed by the news of someone they love, or admire, or follow, but never knew or likely ever met, dies. The cult of saints in the history of Christianity might be a close analogy, but what we are seeing in popular religious cultures now is something that seems quite unique and unprecedented.

The constant and increasing barrage of news about celebrities dying, and the curious responses of communities of fans who are touched by the death, suggests in rather bold terms that Americans do not deny the reality of death but are inundated by reminders of its inevitable truth, even more so now than ever before, and at a hyper-accelerated speed thanks to popular cultures and social media that matter more than families, religious traditions, and other conventional forms of community for providing information about, and the resources needed to make sense of, death.

And, I would argue, these are not superficial distractions nor meaningless entanglements, but where the most real engagements with death are taking place, and spurring Americans to thoughtful religious reflections. The Puritans zeroed in on the corpse to help make sense of death in the community and individual conscience in early New England; today in America, virtual communities with real bonds are united in death and in shared social media ritual expressions of effervescent grief.

You don't need a corpse to take death seriously or be reminded of its "true" reality. Even if the story of death in the last fifty years is, in part, the disappearance of the dead body from public view—embalming, cremations, memorializations—that doesn't necessarily indicate a state of denial or avoidance. Indeed, the public presence and awareness of death has grown over the same time period, thanks in part to the fast-flowing stream of famous people dying.

Contrary to popular belief, America is not now nor has ever been a culture that denies the reality of death. Most of the books about death in America, and certainly the more famous like Mitford's *The American Way of Death*, or Elizabeth Kübler-Ross's *On Death and Dying*, or Ernest Becker's *The Denial of Death*, build their arguments about funerals, dying, and the psyche on the notion that Americans have a peculiar, culturally specific disposition to refuse to accept death. Public discussion and commentaries also tend to reinforce the script as well and perpetuate a longstanding assumption about this supposed unique American trait.

It's a lie. We love death, are obsessed with it, can't get enough of it. Sadly, America is not unique or special — it is like every human culture which, at their roots, provide the conceptual and material tools to live with and think about death. Death work is the essential work of culture, religious work at its core, since it provides the keys to life and its meaning, whether it is through the universal struggle to make sense of suffering, or aging, or health, or identity, or community, or the body. In our time, we see an investment in death at work in medical advancements and enlivening entertainments, political discourses and technological aspirations. In other times and other places, the cultural arenas for death work might focus more on fertilization and agriculture, or astrology and dreams.

We are not alone in trying to live with, explain the reality of, and think appropriately about death. It is one of the few things all humans share and, dare I say, the most urgent and meaningful and powerful human experience that cries out for, and inspires, communal and individual religious actions and ideas — in how the body is disposed of, how the dead are remembered, and how the fate of the spirit is imagined, if it is imagined at all.

The central paradox I've come to realize now, later in my career and in the light of all this enlightenment about cultural patterns and attitudes regarding death in America and globally, is this: when it comes to death, we are social creatures with cultural resources available to help cope with and make sense of death, and at the very same time we are utterly alone in the existential face offs with death that come more frequently with long life.

Family and friends, church or synagogue, social media along with popular cultures—the communities available to so many providing comfort and support, avenues for the expression of grief, and bonding rituals affirming life, are essential to human survival and strength to carry on when individuals die. Death is a social event, one that stands out, is different from other social events because of the emotional impact, the questions raised in the aftermath, and the finality of it.

Over the course of my professional career, this broad awareness and deep knowledge has meant nothing, for the most part, in my own life living with death and dying. My intimacy with death now is more real, less theoretical and abstract than ever; my efforts at intellectualization, at thinking my way through the reality of death via history, anthropology, cultural studies, religion, in the end fails to account for loss, buffer the blows, and salvage meaning as people I have come to know and love die but don't really disappear.

During the last twenty years, death has closed in on me, and each up close and personal encounter seems to build cumulatively with other encounters, so that as I age the weight of those encounters, along with the spirit/memories of the dead that remain alive in my consciousness, sap my efforts at rational understanding. In my case, the more I've studied death, reflected on it, contemplated it, and experienced it more frequently in my life, the more I have come to this realization: It is not the reality of death but the absurdity of this ridiculously short span of time we are alive we must learn to live with, whether you believe there is an eternal soul or nothing. Death doesn't make sense, never arrives at the right time, and is not concerned with justness.

You know I am right, and you can provide your own examples. When my two kids were younger and in school, we experienced two powerful tragedies that could not be fully explained yet clearly marked the lives of all those connected with the decedents. First, a family of four we came to know very well during the elementary school years all died in a small aircraft accident. The news got to us during my second sabbatical while we were living on Victoria Island in Canada, and I was writing the final chapter of *Sacred Matters*, the one on death. We did not go to the funeral, but instead the four of us spontaneously improvised our own ceremony on a small mountaintop with a beautiful view of the Pacific, throwing four flowers to the wind, saying a few words about the family, and feeling both love and sorrow.

A few years later, as my kids were moving into high school, one of the most beloved teachers who must have been in his early forties, died suddenly and unexpectedly. My kids thought he was fantastic, and when we met at one of the school functions early in the term, I thoroughly enjoyed our interactions and conversations, though he appeared a bit wired and wide-eyed to me as well. The cause of death was never publicly announced though we did hear fairly soon after news of his death surfaced that this favorite teacher, husband, father of young kids, took his own life. He had a large funeral service at a Catholic Church, with lots of family, friends, colleagues, and current and former students. To this day I think about him, our conversations, the rumors, his eyes, and wonder with a deep sadness why he did it.

The circumstances of death are ugly and cruel for many people, even as death is made beautiful through various methods like embalming and an open casket, or a fitting memorial service with no body visible at all, or the promises of heavenly reunion in the afterlife. The ravages that come with embodiment before the death of the body, inflicted by disease, violence, aging, and so on, can be unbearable, or at least staggering and disorienting, to those watching death take over and vanquish what's left of a loved family member or friend.

More recently, one of my closest friends from graduate school, died suddenly and at a relatively young age in his early 50s, someone who struggled with alcohol and whose bodily deterioration in the last year and inability to overcome the demon death-bringer that alcohol became for him ensured an early demise. We had been texting as usual over the course of several days when he stopped responding and went silent. I knew something had happened and learned shortly after that he was found dead in his condominium a few days after our final correspondence.

Luís León is gone but remains a part of me, a spectral presence through social media remnants and video snippets, but also somehow as a vital, interior spark in my mind through his writings and especially his first book, *La Llorona's Children: Religion, Life, and Death in the US-Mexico Borderlands*, as obsessed with death and the haunting presences of the dead as my first book.

Death is close at hand and keeps coming, for others and for me eventually. No death is easy, none the same, and nothing so far compares to living with my mother's dying over the course of a few years from cancers that slowly, then quickly at the end, destroyed her body and will to live. I guess I'm going to backtrack on my previous statement—maybe, in many ways, many deaths are similar in America today. I don't think what my mom went through, a difficult death from cancer, is uncommon, and in fact from what I've read and heard from friends, and what we all know to be true but don't talk much about, is that the current healthcare mess is especially hard on the processes and realities of dying for American families across the country.

I wish I could nicely package what she and we went through in a coherent narrative, a story that has a beginning, middle, and end, and which conveys some insight, or clear meaning that emerges in the storytelling of event following event following event. But for me, even three years later, the story is not coherent, and it seems it can only be told in fragments and distortions that are hard to put in words and doesn't really follow any chronology. There are multiple diagnoses from numerous specialist doctors over the course of many years, and so many medical tests; incredible amounts of prescription drugs consumed—pages and pages at the time of her death, and some started earlier, then stopped, so ultimately difficult to calculate, or comprehend; hospital visits, some planned and others emergencies, with my dad by her side always, either behind the wheel driving her or in the ambulances, during the light of day or under the California night sky.

She had top-notch doctors, and kind and humane nurses as the end drew near, so it could have been worse. She never went in to hospice, so my dad was her constant and compassionate caregiver. I visited her frequently—not enough in my own retrospective and tear-soaked assessments—and talked regularly on the phone when she felt up for it, which was less and less often in that last year.

During one of my final visits, when I was getting ready to leave and went to the bedroom to say goodbye, she was laying on her side, facing the wall. I went to her and her face lit up as it always did when we saw each other, and she raised up her arms to hug and kiss me. We embraced and as I moved away from her, I saw that death was with her, clearly on her face and emanating from her body. I saw it and felt it and intuited it and knew it like nothing I have ever known before. I knew it would be the last time I saw her alive, and it was.

I returned back to Atlanta and continued teaching my "Death and Dying" class, which during that semester broke enrollment records with 275 students. My mom was dying as I was teaching that semester, an experience I imagined every time I taught the course over the years—what would happen if someone I loved died while teaching "Death and Dying"?—and one I finally and inevitably lived through. I did not tell the students my mom was dying, and only missed a couple of sessions—one on near-death experiences, and one exploring cross-cultural approaches to end-of-life care.

When I received the phone call that my mom was back in the hospital, and the morphine had been started, and that she likely did not have much longer, I got back on a plane and flew from Atlanta to San Francisco, where I met my brother. We drove from the Bay Area to the Sacramento suburbs as fast as we could, predictably slowed up by California freeway traffic and lots of highway patrol cars. But it wasn't meant to be. She died as we were driving there, hearing the news together over the car sound system from my dad who was as always by her side, now with her body in the hospital room.

We got to the room after seeing my dad pacing the hallway. He and my brother stayed at the doorway and I immediately went to her side. The doctor allowed the body to remain in the hospital bed until we got there, so the three of us were there with her and without her, her body signaling a difficult, painful transition out of this life. I kissed her forehead and cried my eyes out for a while. My mind could not process but my heart knew the immensity of this loss.

Quickly that body was no more. Following her wishes to be cremated rather than be embalmed and put on display or have any kind of grandiose funeral, we arranged with a local funeral home for cremation, then collected the ashes and helped my dad place them in his backyard Zen garden. With me their son, you can guess my parents and I talked for many, many years about my research and teaching, so they had given end of life decisions much thought, and we knew my mom's wishes. We also held a memorial service for her a few weeks later, with some relatives and more recent friends coming together for food and stories.

My two young adult sons were with us at her memorial. As their father, you can imagine how often the topic of death came up on the home front when they were growing up. We talked quite a bit as my mom was dying, and they were aware of the battle with the cancers, the highs and lows of healthcare, the wear and tear and love of my dad, and so on. We also grappled together with other questions, more existential in nature, about the meaning of it all, what we think about religion in it all, and if it all has a purpose.

They were older than I was when my grandparents started dying, and their intimacy with and knowledge about death as teenagers becoming adults was, I think, diametrically opposed to my experiences. Because of increasing longevity overall during the last fifty to seventy-five years, grandparents are living longer, and grandkids I imagine are experiencing their deaths later in life, when they are just entering into young adulthood. During my first twenty-one years of life, even after the deaths of close grandparents, we never as a family talked about or thought together about death. We went to funerals and saw very close family friends die, but other than that conversation I had as a little tyke with the rabbi, who told me not to think about death, my only intellectual, or thoughtful, engagement with the topic came through popular culture.

My mom's memorial service, or "celebration of life" if you prefer the more recent parlance around body-less mortuary rituals, gave momentary public and collective expression to what everyone who met her knew — she was a loving, generous, and uplifting human to be around. Many of the friends and relatives who knew her best and for the longest time were dead, and some too old to make the trip. But still, my dad enjoyed hearing the reminiscences, seeing the room full of people, and experiencing the love for her in the room. The lovely people who came to the celebration were mostly elderly, frail, in bad health, widowed, and near death themselves, though a few longtime friends of me and my brother were there too.

My sons heard me speak, through some tears and vocal stammering, about my love for my mom, how ill-equipped I was to face it even with decades of death-focused studies under my belt, and how, if there is one thing I have learned, is that we all must try to accept our shared fate, that we all must go, eventually. Then I quoted lyrics from *On and On and On* by the band Wilco, a song I played in my "Death and Dying" class as soon as I returned to the classroom, though the students didn't know the true motivation behind our listening. It includes the lyrics:

Please don't cry
We're designed to die
You can't deny
Even the gentlest tide

A few months after my mom's celebration of life after her death, I received an unexpected but wonderfully-timed invitation from an old Japanese scholar friend to attend a special, Buddhist-organized Memorial Day celebration on the beach in Hawaii, a lantern floating ceremony when the living write messages to the dead and send them out to sea. I had not talked for a long time to my dear friend, so he had no idea that my mom had died recently, and I was grieving heavily.

Once again, my death work brought me a strange yet wonderful life opportunity. As one of two scholars invited to the event that draws upwards of fifty thousand people from all over the world, I was asked to attend, participate if I like, and write about the massive public ritual for the dead that has grown in size and popularity over the years for Shinnyo-en Buddhists, whose founder initiated the first lantern floating ceremony in 2002, but more importantly for Buddhists of all stripes, non-Buddhists, Christians, Jews, atheists, Hindus, spiritual but not religious types, native Hawaiian religious cultures, the American military—you get the picture. It is an impressive display of diversity unified by mortality. Sending messages to the dead on handmade, floating, recyclable lit lanterns in a beautiful bay on the beach at sunset is a religious ritual we can all get behind. It was a stunning sight.

The totality of the ritual death spectacle was too much to think about as I sat in my chair on the beach watching the lead-up activities—dancing, music, sermons, chanting, testimonials, multimedia—to the main event, which was taking off your shoes, walking into the surf, and launching your written, illuminated words of love and loss, hope and connection, into the sea.

I sent a message on a lantern out in the ocean to my mom, which surprised me since I'm one who tends to stay far, far away from actually participating in the religious rituals I am studying or thinking about. I remained engaged though a bit detached, trying to observe and identify what I needed to remember so that I could write something relevant, but not too personal. My shoes came off, I walked in the water, and my own hobbled lantern with very unmemorable words of love and sorrow, left my fingers and bobbed away with thousands of other messages to the dead. What do I remember most from that day and evening? Nothing intellectual, but an impression of the deep feelings of love and sorrow I felt I shared with others. We share death. Night came.

The next day I lazed around most of the morning but took a long walk in the park and along the bay where the previous night's festivities and connections occurred. It was empty, for the most part—some joggers and walkers, someone smoking a joint behind a nearby tree, families setting up camp on the sand, some homeless people. I wanted to relive the sharing bonds of love through death with others, but I was alone with my thoughts and a few strangers.

By later afternoon I decided to wander to the Waikiki strip and the crowded shops and beaches and streets and bars. People were everywhere, which I thought would be an anodynic distraction before returning home the following morning, No work, no grief, no death, at least for a few hours.

When I walked across the strip to get to a beachside bar, someone stopped me out of the blue and started talking with me about the weather, the beauty of the island, and how crowded it was in Waikiki.

I looked at the young woman who approached me and was momentarily taken aback by her decision to stop and begin talking with me. She was a good three or four inches taller than me and had to look down in our conversation, while I conversed looking up over my sunglasses and into her eyes.

"You know you have beautiful eyes," she said within minutes of our meeting. That's when she really threw me off by asking me if I was looking for company. Given that the whole trip to Hawaii was surreal from the get-go, I thought to myself, "What the hell," and said to her, "Sure, let's go get a drink."

When we walked into the bar, an old, grey-haired man with a tall, dirty blond young woman, I began to notice all the fun-loving and good-natured beach bums around the bar stare at the two of us with inquisitive and questioning and knowing looks. I also finally fully realized what "company" meant in her question. I may have a PhD and an endowed chair, but the truth is I can be a complete idiot sometimes. But in my defense, this was an entirely novel situation for me, and now I didn't want to be rude to a fellow human being who, by whatever circumstances conspired to bring her to this moment, had agreed with the proposition that we spend some time together. And I was in the mood for a drink.

We found a place at the bar, sat down, and ordered. I never got her name but she ordered a double margarita and, for some reason, I thought mezcal would be appropriate for the moment. We continued with some small talk for a short bit, and then she asked: "So, what are you doing here in Hawaii?" I looked at her, took a deep breath, and took a slow gulp of the mezcal. Luckily the bartender came up to us right as I was finishing and asked how we were doing, which gave me another moment to get it together.

"Do you really want to know?" I asked. She nodded. At this point I knew how the night was going to end—me heading back to my hotel alone after our drinks—and pondered whether to just lie completely about my presence in this paradise, or tell the truth, go back to what I thought I was getting away from in my social excursion with the living, and bring "it" up. In reality there was no question about my response, since I don't like to lie too much and I saw this as my duty as a "public scholar."

"Well actually, to be honest, I'm here to be in the company of the dead." The look on her face was priceless. After a bit of silence her face lit up, she smiled, and took a long sip from her plastic straw while looking me straight in the eyes. "Sounds intriguing. Tell me more." I gave her some of the background to the ceremony, my experience as a special guest, and a brief description of who attended.

"So you're a Buddhist? A lot of my friends like to meditate, and we all love that really old, funny, sweet man in robes . . . the Dali Lama. That's it, right?" "Yes, that's the old man," I averred. "But I'm no Buddhist. Believe it or not, I'm a professor and study religion, and a very kind friend invited me to be a guest at the ceremony this year."

That opened up the familiar conversation that tends to come up whenever I try to explain what I do. We moved through the usual touchstones: yes, I study religion, but no, I'm not rabbi; yes, I study religion, but no, I don't believe in God; yes, I study religion, but no, I'm not interested in training future rabbis or ministers. It's a conversation I've had many times yet it really never grows old for me since most people have no idea, and I get a kick out of fooling with religion, especially during spontaneous conversations that come up with strangers on a plane, for example, or with a mystery woman at a bar.

I also opened up another can of worms and let her know of my extensive and peculiar engagement with the topic of death—books, articles, blogs, posts, interviews, classes. The whole shebang. It was clear that she is quite intelligent and seems genuinely interested in delving even deeper into the topics of death, religion, and "the big questions," which is what, in fact, I do for a living.

"My mom died when I was a young kid," she revealed suddenly. I could tell she was not going to cry but that obviously a deep pain had surfaced. "I only recently moved here from Iowa. My dad is a complete asshole. Talk about religious nut cases. He is one for sure, and he loves Trump, which makes me sick. So, I had to get out of there. Some friends helped me get here," she said, and then took another long drink.

I felt a great deal of sympathy for her but could tell she did not want me to pursue any further, so I mentioned that my mom had died recently and that, while I had a professional and intellectual interest in the ceremony, the timing seemed rather serendipitous for strongly personal and existential reasons. The timing could not have been better, quite frankly—in the wake of my mom's death, on a national holiday that mourns and remembers the dead, and at the very end of a particularly killer semester.

As I was sitting on my stool, surrounded by loud, boisterous Hawaii-loving patrons, staring eye to eye with a hooker and talking about "existential" this, and "intellectual" that, about our dead mothers, about time and timing, about our religious sensibilities, I was struck by the utter absurdity of the moment. But I loved being in that moment. And I loved the mezcal. I think my bar companion was loving her double margarita too.

"I believe in reincarnation," she confessed. "I think after we die we're born again, not in the Christian sense, but that we are really brought back and get to live again. And hopefully you learn from mistakes and your lives get better and better." That would be nice, I thought to myself. We sat in silence for a bit before she looked at me dead in the eye and asked, point blank:

"Why do you think so much about death?"

Part Two: Writings

1.

The Body Politic and the Politics of Two Bodies: Abraham And Mary Todd Lincoln in Death

A braham Lincoln has been mythologized and deified in the American imagination, occupying a preeminent place in the collective memory of the nation. He occupies this place because he is believed to embody the ideals and values of the country and because he seemed to preside with grace, equanimity, and wisdom over one of the most destructive conflicts in America's history. In life, but even more consequently in death, his presence— as "rail splitter," "Great Emancipator," and "Father Abraham"- conjures up an array of events, symbols, and myths that give definition and meaning to the American nation.

When he died, an unprecedented funeral celebration occurred in the Northern region of the United States that solidified his privileged place in the country's pantheon of great heroes. The series of events that took place after his assassination, as well as his emplotment in public memory since then, suggest that his death, as tragic and painful as it was, added to the cohesion, unity, and the very life of the nation when it was most seriously threatened by chaos and degeneration.[1]

Lincoln's assassination took place at the end of a war that divided the country in two, threatened the very existence of American society, and claimed the lives of roughly six-hundred thousand men.[2] In the midst of Northern celebrations, the deathblow created an unparalleled crisis that forced Union leaders and supporters to address the grief, mourning, and disorientation following in its wake. The display of Lincoln's body during the funeral journey not only concentrated the attention of Northerners on the price of victory and the perceived righteousness of the Union cause, it also literally fixed their gaze on the exhibition of a traveling, embalmed corpse — something most of them had never seen before.[3] In the larger public arena, the journey of the body and the spectacle of its presentation gave Northern political and religious figures the opportunity of reimagining the sacrality and meaning of the social body after its near dissolution. The symbolism of the Union was grafted onto the symbolism of his traveling body, allowing leaders in the North to link such religious themes as national integrity, collective redemption, and millennial destiny to the disposal of his remains.

What can Lincoln's corpse, and the actions and words surrounding its burial, tell Americans that they do not already know — or that they even want to know? As many cultural and social historians and anthropologists have discovered, the dead are extraordinarily revealing objects of inquiry because so many discourses — religious, medical, economic, political, and so on — are inscribed on the remains between the moment of death and final disposition.[4] While practices used in the disposal of the dead usually perpetuate forms of social organization that reinforce hierarchical power structures (the poor being buried anonymously in potter's fields, the righteous in the sacred soil of the church, the persecuted in a state of desecration and defilement, etc.), the burial of culturally significant individuals can be a critical time for group solidarity; the very principles, aspirations, and ideals that animate the society in which that person lived must be carefully articulated and must reaffirm the logic of the ties that bind individuals together.[5]

Clearly the collective practices and imaginative strategies that account for death often reflect the shared values and common symbols of those societal members left behind. In Lincoln's case, the series of ritual and discursive practices that took place after his assassination ensured that his death served the public rhetoric of religious nationalism emanating from Northern Protestant culture. On the other hand, conflicts over meaning and disagreements over placement that occasionally surround the dead, and often emerge from the periphery of the social order, tell a different story. These contests challenge the hegemonic narratives constructed at the time of death and bear more on identity formation and power divisions within a community than on the reaffirmation of an established social order. For these reasons, the body of Abraham Lincoln—as it was being physically ushered out of society—demands the historian's attention; though his corpse was abundant with meaning and ultimately fit into a mythic American narrative, between the time of death and burial it was also riddled with multiple layers of symbolism that were not always compatible with the collective, public process of memorialization.[6]

Unfortunately for Mary Todd Lincoln, the entire country was emotionally invested in the activities that accompanied her husband's corpse on its funeral journey to Springfield, Illinois—the nation's very survival seemed to depend on the body's smooth transition out of the land of the living. The president's public position as "head" of state—especially after the destruction inflicted on the social body during four years of fighting superseded his private role as father or husband when his remains were laid to rest. His corpse, like no other during the war (or perhaps for all of American history), had to convey a message of national regeneration, social cohesion, and hope for the future; politicians and religious leaders expressed a distinctly religious vision of the nation that required the body to help soothe the collective suffering of the people in the North. For Mary Todd, on the other hand, the body of her husband could not be defined solely in its relation to the State. It also belonged in the more private, personal sphere of the Lincoln family, where she participated in the domestic system of symbols and meanings associated with death. For this reason, she was determined to remain involved in deciding the fate of her husband's corpse. Her struggles to control the body, and her relationship to it, bring the story of Lincoln's death back down to earth, where the politics of gender, nationalism, and the family determined its ultimate meaning.

THE "SLOW DEATH" OF MARY TODD LINCOLN

By the time Abraham Lincoln assumed the presidency in 1861, Mary Todd had already been recognized by many as a troublesome, difficult woman.[7] She had a reputation for intruding in her husband's affairs and entering an arena many thought women did not belong: politics. While she claimed to be only interested in the domestic sphere of the Lincoln family, her personal commitment to and public actions in support of Abraham's political career made her a marked woman.[8] Her first four years in the White House only increased her notoriety as a public figure, especially when it came to her spending habits and influence on her husband's political appointments. As Jean Baker, one of Mary Todd's recent biographers suggests, the president's wife lived in two worlds that were considered separate in the 19th century, the private and the public: "Throughout her four years in Washington, Mary Lincoln inhabited both the male sphere of public affairs and the females secluded habitat."[9]

In addition to these areas of criticism, the first "First Lady" had another vulnerable attribute that many exploited both during her years in the White House and after her husband's death: her Southern heritage. Born and raised in the South, Mary Todd attained national prominence at the moment the two regions of the country split apart. Most of her relatives in Lexington, Kentucky, supported secession as soon as the war began, and a number of family members were killed fighting for the Rebels. Journalists, politicians, and other individuals in and around Washington who disliked the president's wife contributed to rumors that she sympathized with the Confederate cause because of her family roots. Although she did not stay in close contact with many of these relations after marriage and had numerous defenders who tried to counter the charges, Mary Todd could not escape the persistent accusations that she secretly harbored Southern loyalties and was a threat at the very center of Union power.[10] As difficult and as painful as these attacks were against Mary Todd, her experiences after the murder led to even greater suffering and personal disgrace.

In the weeks after the assassination, Lincoln's corpse became visible and accessible to people in the North; from the moment he was shot on Good Friday to the final interment in Springfield, it was considered public property, given to the citizens who made up the Union body politic. On the other hand, as soon as her husband slumped down in the seat next to her, Mary Todd's body became intrusive and problematic; her ultimate destiny was to be severed from American public life and disassociated from the apotheosis of the dead president. While Abraham Lincoln moved to the center of national consciousness, the widow received less and less respect and receded from public view—occasionally on her own terms. In addition to being absent during the civic ceremonies for her husband, she refused to abandon the mourning clothes that set her apart from the rest of society and decided to distance herself from the United States during two exiles; on the other hand, the media and various politicians frequently humiliated her in public, and about ten years after the death, her own son forced her to enter an insane asylum.

Moments after John Wilkes Booth shot the president in the back of the head at Ford's Theater on Good Friday, April 14, 1865, Mary Todd became inconsolable and pleaded with her husband to speak; when volunteers took her mortally wounded husband to a house across the street, she was removed from the room where they placed the body so it could be examined by the attending physicians and carefully watched.[11] As her husband lingered on the verge of death, Mary Todd sat in a separate room down the hall, periodically visiting the deathbed and upsetting the men who surrounded the dying president. Her emotional disposition annoyed the reserved, self-controlled men congregated around the body, leading one of them — possibly War Secretary Edwin M. Stanton — to exclaim, "Keep that woman out of here."[12] Before the president finally expired on the morning of the fifteenth, Mary Todd Lincoln was reported to have anticipated his death.

The Lincoln's eldest son, Robert, led his mother to a house that belonged to "the people," a dream home that became a nightmare for the widow. At the White House, Mary Todd did not spend much time, if any, with her husband's body. She stayed in a small, spare room where she continued to moan, sob, and rest.[13] Fortunately, a few close and trusted allies visited and consoled the grieving widow, reaffirming her spiritualist leanings with assurances that Abraham was close at hand and watching over her and the family.[14] By the very next day, Easter Sunday, workers began to build a catafalque in the East Room that would hold the coffin of the dead president during the funeral ceremony. Even though she was greatly disturbed by all the commotion, and especially the hammering that reminded her of the pistol shot that killed her husband, Mary Todd refused to leave her room. A request was made to suspend all the necessary activity, but the preparations continued. Her private torment and grief were secondary to the more important public response of the federal government, which had to demonstrate its sorrow with greater composure, formality, and national purpose. Although Mary Todd was aware of all the activity taking place in the White House, she was too emotionally distraught to participate in the funeral ceremonies in Washington or in any of the rituals that were performed during the course of the funeral journey.

The funeral train bound for Springfield carried the remains of her dead husband as well as the remains of their third son, Willie, who had died a few years earlier in the midst of war. After the funeral train departed for Springfield, Mary Todd continued her seclusion in the White House. One of the first developments to bring Mary Todd from out of her sorrowful anguish, however, was the question of where her husband's body would be finally located. Within hours of the assassination, city council members in Springfield began to arrange for the disposal of the president's remains in their city, purchasing six acres at its very center. They believed that Springfield was Lincoln's true home and that his body should be placed in a public space in the town where he began his political career, close to old friends and neighbors.

Mary Todd's initial two choices were Chicago and Washington, D.C., but she soon recalled that on a recent trip to the James River, near City Point, her husband—who was confident that he would die before his wife—asked her to make sure his remains were buried in a setting similar to the quiet and peaceful land along the James. She also remembered how taken he was with the new Oak Ridge "rural" cemetery in Springfield.

With the funeral journey moving from one city to the next, Mary Todd finally decided to place her husband's body in Oak Ridge, despite the wishes of organizers and politicians in Springfield. The widow demanded and ultimately received what she desired: that she and other family members be allowed to rest with him in death. While the public might claim his traveling embalmed body as their own, she would fight to safeguard the eternal integrity of the domestic, family unit in which Abraham Lincoln was husband and father first and national martyr second. She clearly understood and encouraged the sacred status her husband had assumed at the time of his death, but she refused to allow the president's remains to be appropriated and controlled by public officials who demonstrated little concern for her desires and an insensitive disregard for the family ties linking the president to a smaller, more intimate circle of relations.[15] Mary Todd did not leave the White House until May 23, over a month after her husband's murder. Covered from head to toe in black mourning garb, she was escorted out by a small group of family, friends, and officials. Elizabeth Keckley, Mary Todd's assistant, confidante, and eventual enemy, described in her memoirs the loneliness and isolation of the widow when she departed the White House: "I can never forget that day; it was so unlike the day when the body of the President was borne from the hall in grand and solemn state. Then thousands gathered to bow the head in reverence as the plumed hearse drove down the line…Now, the wife of the President was leaving the White House, and there was scarcely a friend to tell her good-by…The silence was almost painful."[16]

There may have been a silence surrounding the departure of the former First Lady, but the very day she left, the nation's capitol was having an official celebration commemorating the victory over the South—Union troops paraded down Pennsylvania Avenue in full force, cheered on by relieved and adoring Northerners.[17]

Mary Todd eventually decided to make her new residence in Chicago, rejecting the suggestion that she return to Springfield and the home where she and her family once lived. In addition to the overwhelming number of memories that would make her existence unbearable, she had a good number of enemies in the city—particularly after her refusal to turn over the president's remains. From the time she left the White House until her own death in 1882, Mary Todd's life was filled with alienation, defeats, and tragedies. She literally could not find a stable place in society, living mostly in hotels, with close relations, and in foreign countries for the rest of her life. In the years following the assassination, she was publicly attacked for a number of reasons, including alleged financial improprieties, supposed mental instability, and a particularly cutting smear from Lincoln's old law partner, William Herndon, that she was not, in fact, the former president's true love. As the nation grew in strength as a result of the memory of the dead president, Mary Todd's physical condition deteriorated and her mental faculties were increasingly called into question by others.

One of the most damaging incidents to the widow's reputation, and an episode that greatly contributed to her decision to leave the country, was what became known as the "Old Clothes Scandal." Desperate for money and feeling abandoned by the federal government, Mary Todd decided to sell some of her more luxurious clothes and jewelry. The plan turned into a complete failure and ultimately led to the worst kind of public embarrassment for her. The brokers who agreed to sell her items came up with a scheme to exhibit her belongings in different cities and charge for admission. Included in the exhibit would be the bloodstained clothes the president's wife wore at the time of the assassination. Although the organizers did not consult Mary Todd and she never approved of the plan, the press and many prominent politicians derided her and made accusations that she was greedy, unscrupulous, and simply insane. With the publication of the revealing *Behind the Scenes* by Keckley in the Spring of 1868—a breach of friendship that was devastating to Mary Todd—the widow of the glorified president decided to leave what she called "this ungrateful Republic" and sail to Europe with her youngest son, Tad.[18]

From 1868 to 1871, Mary Todd and her son lived in and traveled through Europe and Great Britain, seeking to escape from the hard, distressing life they had to endure in the States after the assassination. Despite opposition from close friends and family, Mary Todd believed that the change would be beneficial to Tad's education as well as her own mental and physical health; she pursued her interest in spiritualism and the endeavor to overcome the rupture between the living and the dead,[19] and she tried new therapies for a series of physical symptoms—including migraines, chills, and feebleness of limbs—that most of her doctors associated with "nervous disorders" unique to middle and upper-class women. Even Mary Todd herself referred to her ailments as a consequence of her "womanly nature."[20]

While she was away trying to heal herself and take care of her son, persistent rumors questioned her sanity and challenged her status in American society—there was even talk that she planned to marry a foreign dignitary.[21] Mary Todd resolved some of the ambiguities surrounding her unique position as the first widow of a murdered president, however, during her time outside of the country. Three years after Congress introduced a bill, she secured a widow's pension for herself though vigorous support by a few advocates, including Senator Charles Sumner, was critical to her success. The debate over this bill stirred up another round of abuse by politicians and the media, who questioned her patriotism and fidelity to her husband. [22]

Upon their return to the States in 1871, Tad grew sick and died—another crushing blow to Mary Todd's emotional and physiological condition. With this last death, Mary Todd had seen three of her four sons die—Eddie in 1850, Willie in 1862, and now Tad—and her husband murdered by an assassin's bullet. She conveyed the utter devastation in her life after Tad's death in a letter, writing that "my heart is entirely broken, for without his presence, the world is complete darkness."[23]

Unfortunately, things would get worse for Mary Todd. In the years that followed Tad's death, she continued to make efforts to heal her pain by traveling to health spas and attending spiritualist seances. She even had a "spirit photograph" taken of herself in which the reassuring presence of Abraham Lincoln, hands on each of her shoulders, face solemnly looking down from above, stood behind her seated figure. Despite this image of her husband's presence in her life, though, the public had already established an iconography of the dead president that did not include her or any members of his family. He was often paired with the reigning divine image of the country, George Washington, or appeared in more idiosyncratic representations, including Erastus Salisbury Field's painting, *Historical Monument of the American Republic* (ca. 1876), where he is prepared by angels for his ascension to heaven.[24]

Four years after Tad's death, her only remaining son, Robert, requested that his mother be certified as a lunatic and put away in an insane asylum for her own benefit. On the day of the trial, seventeen people, including hotel employees, physicians, and Robert himself, testified. The witnesses focused on her shopping habits and physical condition, as well as her apparent nervous condition, hallucinations, paranoia, and other forms of what they considered to be irrational behavior. In a summary of the evidence against her, the May 20, 1875, *New York Times* reported, "Several witnesses testified to eccentricities in the conduct of Mrs. Lincoln, which commenced at the time of the assassination of President Lincoln, and which have become more marked as time progressed. She imagines she hears voices in the wall, that strange beings beset her in the entries of her hotel, that she was the victim of poisoning plots, etc. Her closets are full of unopened packages of goods which she had ordered to be sent to her room."[25] The statements by the various physicians carried significant weight during the trial, with one claiming that Mary Todd expressed a belief that an "Indian spirit" was involved in malevolent actions in her head.[26]

Robert initiated these proceedings after his mother accused him of plotting to murder her. During the hearing, he expressed his own conclusions to the jurors about his mother's mental state and unusual behavior (with a special focus on her habit of overextending herself when shopping): "I have no doubt my mother is insane. She has long been a source of great anxiety to me. She has no home and no reason to make these purchases."[27]

With little help from her own attorney, Mary Todd's fate was sealed when the all-male jury deliberated for ten minutes and returned with a verdict of insanity. The reporter for the *New York Times* described what took place after the decision: "At the commencement of the verdict, Robert Lincoln took the hand of his mother affectionately, when she exclaimed, with reproachful tone, 'Oh, Robert, to think that my son would ever have done this.'"[28] After a reported suicide attempt, she was admitted to a sanitarium for women in Batavia, Illinois.[29]

In a little over a year, Mary Todd was judged as sane and released from the care of sanitarium doctors, thanks to the efforts of close friends and relatives and her own exemplary behavior while in the institution. She lived for a while in Springfield and then embarked on another journey to the continent, again to seek out peace and tranquility in the anonymity of European society. This exile lasted four years. In 1880, Mary Todd had to return to the United States because of failing health and the inability to live on her own. Two years later, she suffered a stroke and died. Her well attended funeral took place in Springfield three days after her demise. It was only on this occasion, at the time of her death, that she was, in the words of biographer Jean Baker, "returned...to female respectability as a loyal wife" by a society that had difficulty accepting her from the moment she became a public figure.[30]

There were communal displays of mourning and collective acts of sorrow on the day of the funeral, and Robert, the only remaining member of the Lincoln family, led the funeral procession. In his funeral sermon in the First Presbyterian Church, the Reverend James A. Reed compared the Lincolns to two pine trees, roots and branches intertwined as they grew toward the sky. When one was struck down, the other appeared to be unscathed but, Reed continued, "they had virtually both been killed at the same time. With the one that lingered it was slow death from the same cause. So it seems to me today, that we are only looking at death placing his seal upon the lingering victim of a past calamity."[31] When the service ended, the body of Mary Todd Lincoln was placed in a burial vault next to her husband and three sons.[32]

THE VISIBILITY OF ABRAHAM LINCOLN'S BODY

The funeral for Abraham Lincoln ended twenty days after the assassination. Although Mary Todd had to wait until her own death to be publicly reunited with her husband, Northern leaders immediately detached the body of the president from the domestic circle of his family during its journey to Springfield. In speeches and sermons throughout the North, prominent religious figures and politicians used the display of his body as an opportunity to remind all who were listening about the sacred quality of the nation and to insert the sixteenth president into the pantheon of great national heroes.

While the public grew more and more distant from the widow's troubled and indecorously mourning body over the course of her life, the president's translucent and legible body was prepared for and exposed to the scrutiny of the masses in the North and Washington, D.C. The funeral train carrying the remains stopped in many of the major urban centers in the North, including Philadelphia, New York, and Chicago, to bring the people into contact with the fallen martyr.

The Southern states, of course, had no access to Lincoln, especially because many thought the Confederate government was involved in the murder. A number of Northern religious ministers who were leaning toward forgiveness and mercy prior to Booth's action called for swift and forceful punishment against Southern leaders and other guilty parties after it.[33] But Southern reaction to the death and funeral of Lincoln was characterized by extremes. On the one hand, a genuine expression of outrage and sadness arose in many areas of the region when news of the president's death reached the South. On the other hand, suspicions about the people in the Southern states were confirmed by a willingness on the part of certain individuals to applaud publicly the crime and call for national celebrations.[34]

Some newspapers praised the murder in the name of patriotism, including the *Daily Constitutionalist* based in Augusta, Georgia. When it reported on what was thought to be a double murder (of Lincoln and Secretary of State, William Seward), the column referred to the two men as "the two archfiends of the revolution" and described how "all Yankeedom mourns and howls over the discomfiture of its two leading tyrants."[35] The South was clearly no place to send the body of the president in order to enhance the possibilities of sectional reconciliation and a truly national process of mourning, but the federal government attempted a symbolic rehabilitation of the entire nation through a westward tour in the North.

In the nation's capital, the public accessibility to Lincoln's body began almost instantly. Roughly twenty-five soldiers, doctors, and bystanders took the mortally wounded president from the theater to a room across the street.[36] Numerous men moved in and out of the small room where the president was to die, including family, friends, doctors, and politicians; his body was always in their sights, and every breath, sound, or facial expression subject to their analysis. At the moment of death, some of the men cried, though the majority of them remained silent. A few moments after Lincoln died, the Rev. Dr. Phineas Gurley was asked to say something. He responded by making an appeal that "we and the whole nation might become more than ever united in our devotion to the cause of our beloved, imperiled country."[37]

Before the body could be given over to the people as a symbol of this national unity, it had to be taken apart and then reassembled for public presentation. Although the majority of corpses were handled by family members and close relatives or friends before the onset of the war, the president's body was immediately put under the control of professionals who specialized in death and the dead. Their scrutiny of the body's interior and manipulation of its appearance foreshadowed the hegemonic position death specialists (i.e., doctors and funeral directors) have in our own day.[38] Doctors from the newly created Army Medical Museum performed an autopsy on the body in the Guest Room on the second floor of the White House; during this examination, the top of the president's head was sawed off and the brain removed. As the surgeons withdrew the brain, the bullet that had been lodged there fell onto the floor.[39] At the conclusion of the autopsy, the embalming of the body began.

Undertakers working with the firm of Brown and Alexander, the same firm employed by the Lincolns' when Willie died, commenced to drain the blood from the jugular vein.[40] A chemical preparation was then injected through the femoral artery, giving the corpse what some subsequently referred to as a statuesque, marblelike appearance. The postmortem interventions of these specialists, it should be noted, were frequently reported in various newspapers, offering the public information about the technological innovations being discovered in bodily preservation and used on their president. For example, on Saturday, April 22, 1865, the Pittsburgh *Daily Post* printed the following account from a correspondent for the New York *World*:

> There is now no blood in the body, it was drained by the jugular vein and sacredly preserved, and through a cutting on the inside of the thigh, the empty blood-vessels were charged with a chemical preparation which soon hardened to the consistence *[sic]* of stone. The long and bony body is now hard and stiff, so that beyond its present position it cannot be moved any more than the arms or legs of a statue. It has undergone many changes. The scalp has been removed, the brain scooped out, the chest opened and the blood emptied. All this we see of Abraham Lincoln, so cunningly contemplated in this splendid coffin, is a mere shell, an effigy, a sculpture. He lies in sleep, but it is the sleep of marble.[41]

When these specialists were finished with the body, Stanton decided on the clothes the president would wear on his journey—the same black suit he wore for his second inaugural. The coffin was then placed on the elaborate catafalque constructed in the East Room, where reminders of death and sorrow gave material expression to the solemn mood of the North. Black mourning crepe, arrangements of flowers, and greenery surrounded the body; black and white cloth covered the mirrors, and black streamers hung from various locations throughout the room. On Tuesday the eighteenth, the body of the former president was presented to the public. A line stretching over a mile long, six or seven people across, had formed by midmorning. [42] Citizens were allowed to mount the catafalque and file past the body; they were given an opportunity to glance at the face of the sixteenth president and pay their last respects.

The next day was reserved only for people who had special passes to attend the official funeral ceremony. Over five hundred people crowded into the East Room for the religious services—offered by representatives from the Episcopalian, Methodist, Presbyterian, and Baptist churches. All across the North, however, people were engaged in services honoring the dead president—in time, many of them would be able to see the passing funeral train or visit and worship near his remains. [43] Before the funeral train left on its journey, a grand funeral procession transported the body from the White House to the Capitol. With church bells tolling and funeral dirges playing, a black regiment led the hearse and the rest of the cavalcade up Pennsylvania Avenue. At the Capitol the corpse, positioned on another catafalque, was once again given over to the gaze of the public. In the rotunda, all of the paintings on the walls and all of the statues, with the exception of George Washington's, were hidden beneath black crepe.

Finally, on Friday the twenty-first, the funeral train left Washington and headed toward Springfield, making stops in over ten Northern cities. In each city, citizens participated in ceremonies associated with the display of his body, and tens of thousands of people were allowed to view the remains before they left for the next destination. Indeed, in many accounts of the funeral journey, reporters remarked on the unprecedented nature of the public ceremonies in these cities. They also mentioned the large number of people who lined the tracks that carried the remains of Lincoln, as well as the outpouring of sympathy the people expressed watching the train pass. Relatives (with the exception of Mary Todd), close friends, military personnel, and delegates accompanied the corpse on the train. In addition to these people, another important figure traveled with the body all the way to Springfield: the embalmer. Working closely with local undertakers along the way, he made sure it was suitable for public consumption.

Throughout the entire journey, there were conflicting reports about how the body was holding up. Most people remarked on the "peaceful," "placid," or "natural" expression on the face of the president—in some instances leading individuals, mostly women according to reports, to reach out and touch him or even try to kiss his face or the coffin that held his body. In a description offered in the Philadelphia paper, the *Daily Evening Bulletin*, the remains conveyed many of the qualities the president demonstrated when alive: "The countenance still preserved the impression it bore in life, though changed in hue, the lips firmly set but half smiling, and on the whole the face still indicating the energy and humor which characterized the living man." The column went on to state that "all the details were perfect" and commended the work of the embalmers.[44]

In the words of Charles Page, journalist for the *New York Tribune* during the war, "The face of the dead President bears a very natural expression, one familiar to all who saw him often. It is just the hint of a smile, and the look of benediction. I do not know to what it is attributable, but certainly the face is far more natural, more *his*, than when seen four days ago at Washington."[45]

And finally, in an article in the *Indianapolis Daily Journal,* a correspondent wrote, "Although discolored, there is nothing of the repulsiveness of death visible in the dead President's face. The expression is that of calm, placid contentment, as if he were enjoying an untroubled sleep, rather than that of a person who has perished by violence."[46]

Some accounts, on the other hand, contradicted this popular narrative of supernatural tranquility and physical composure. Instead of familiarity and peace, there was something disturbing and chaotic in the facial features of the former president. The strange discoloration beginning to transform his appearance was too dramatic to overlook. In one New York newspaper, a reporter suggested that for those who had never seen the man up close, the view of the remains would be "satisfactory." But, the writer went on to say, "to those who were familiar with his features, it is far otherwise. The color is leaden, almost brown; the forehead recedes sharp and clearly marked;... the cheeks, hollow and deep pitted; the unnaturally thin lips shut tight and firm as if glued together." This journalist was not very optimistic about the future presentability of the corpse because of its continued exposure to the air and its instability aboard a jerking, vibrating train. By the end of the article, the writer questioned whether it was appropriate or prudent—despite the "cunning workmanship"—to "tempt dissolution much further."[47]

The *Cleveland Plain Dealer* reported that the embalming may not have been as effective as others suggested when it was displayed in New York: "From the time the corps *[sic]* was deposited in the City Hall until removed, the appearance of the body indicated that the embalming had not been perfect, discoloration is daily increasing, and it is thought the coffin cannot be opened after leaving the city."[48] Echoing these sentiments, an actress from England also remarked on the apparent failure to preserve the president's corpse adequately. Writing from a hotel in Baltimore nearly one month after the body had passed through, Ellen Kean stated that "there was something very undignified and very shocking...in parading the poor remains about from town to town to gratify the morbid curiosity of the idle, more especially as the process of embalming had been unsuccessful." According to her report, the body had already begun to decay before it left Washington. She went on to say that eventually "they had to resort to the hideous trick of puffing out the cheeks and painting them before they could expose it to view."[49]

Upon reaching Springfield, the body of the former president was clearly beginning to lose the illusion of solidity and tranquility; that statuesque, marblelike appearance was threatened by the inevitable signs of putrefaction. The undertakers who opened the coffin before its exposure to the public were dismayed at what they saw and what they were having difficulty controlling: the increasing darkness in the facial features—especially under the right eye—that signaled decay. Throughout the journey attendants tried to disguise any physical manifestations of death that might appear, but upon the body's arrival in Springfield, it became clear that their efforts were no longer effective.

Frustrated in his attempts to make the body presentable, the traveling embalmer gave in to the request of the local undertaker and let him try to conceal the progress of decomposition. With the help of thick applications of rouge chalk and amber, the undertaker seemed to be able to hide the marked discoloration.[50]

Unfortunately, the applications did not hold when the body was exhibited in the State House the next day. In addition to the usual remarks about his serene countenance and peaceful features, there were also the more candid comments about the wholly unnatural appearance of the face and the disconcerting impression this left with many of those who filed by.[51] But despite the formation of a counternarrative describing the corpse as unworthy of a last look, the president's body had been safely purified and firmly located in the hearts, imagination, and memory of many in the North as a result of its public exhibition—any signs of physical discomposure on the body became secondary to the coherent

85

imaginative body that signified national permanence. This facade of wholeness and integrity that was so critical to the president's memorialization, and to the construction of the nation's self-identity, represented the dominant culture's predilection to gloss over the more distressing signs of physical disintegration and stress symbolic national unity. In spite of what many saw on the decomposing corpse, funeral sermons and political speeches constituted the president's body as an object of worship that could inspire feelings of redemption and social union. In a speech during the New York ceremonies, George Bancroft stated, "His death, which was meant to sever it [the Union] beyond repair, binds it more closely and more firmly than ever. The blow aimed at him was aimed, not at the native of Kentucky, not at the citizen of Illinois, but at the man who, as President, in the executive branch of government, stood as the representative of every man in the United States. From Maine to the southwest boundary on the Pacific it makes us one country."[52]

In a grand, ornate procession on May 4, 1865, a hearse transported the corpse from the State House to Oak Ridge Cemetery. The journey of Lincoln's body was finally over. As Bishop Matthew Simpson of the Methodist Church explained in his funeral oration, though the nation was paralyzed during the "mournful silence" that followed the assassination, the concentrated attention on the president's body not only obliterated all social distinctions — of class, political orientation, faith, and even race — it also encouraged social fellowship and collective renewal. He made it clear that the visibility of the body, the opportunity given to the public to look upon the remains, contributed to this process of healing and rejuvenating the social body.

"Far more eyes have gazed upon the face of the departed than ever looked upon the face of any other departed man ... We ask, why this wonderful mourning — this great procession? I answer, first: A part of the interest has arisen from the times in which we live and in which he that had fallen was a principal actor...Another principal is, that the deepest affections of our hearts gather around some human form, in which are incarnated the living thoughts and ideas of a passing age."[53]

Simpson went on to reiterate a common theme that was expressed during Lincoln's funeral journey: that this body was a vehicle through which God acted in history: "Mr. Lincoln was no ordinary man, and I believe the conviction has been growing on the nation's mind, as it certainly has been on my own, especially in the last years of his administration. By the hand of God he was especially singled out to guide our government in these troublous [sic] times, and it seems to me that the hand of God may be traced in many events connected with his history."[54]

TWO BODIES, TWO SYSTEMS OF MEANING

If it is true that Abraham Lincoln is, as Sidney Mead has argued, "the spiritual center of American history," then the meanings assigned to his death and the ceremonies enacted during his burial must have left their mark on American culture and the political life of the nation.[55] While the Confederacy did not recognize the legitimacy of Lincoln's presidency, for the North his death was a severe threat to national stability and continuity. Lincoln was not a monarch (though many political cartoonists loved to depict him as one), but the impact of his death required a collective response that hinted at his implicit kingly status.[56] For Union ideology, the death of its "king" at the very moment of military victory could not impede the major political reconstitution of the state and instead had to be understood as a propitious sign of continued divine sanction of the national mission. Lincoln's public body—democratized and available to the gaze of Northern citizens—participated in the confirmation of the Union's vision of national meaning.

Mary Todd Lincoln, though referred to as "La Reine" while in the White House and associated with Queen Victoria after the death, did not receive the same kind of royal treatment as the dead president, however. She was disparaged and vilified during her life, and neglected by the Northern community, who did not consider her as "kin" after the death of their leader. Her pathological, "dying" body—associated with national wounds as well as feminine mysteries—did not receive much public sympathy, support, or charity, and the corrosion of her identity was a necessary consequence in the affirmation of national identity. The construction of Mary Todd's living body as irrelevant, disturbing, and disordered contributed to certain meanings encoded in the president's decomposing body by many in the North who preferred to imagine him as a member of the national family rather than as a father and husband in his own family circle.

In death, Lincoln's corpse was inscribed with a variety of significant representational schemes that, contrary to the experiences of most Protestant families in the 19th century, did not depend on its placement within the nuclear family unit. The exhibition of his body added vitality to the Northern religious discourse seeking to rejuvenate the entire country and mend a broken, fragmented body politic.[57] The symbolism linking the corpse with the social body signified at least two orders of meaning. In the first place, there was the existence—indeed the hegemony—of the state in the funeral activities and discourses surrounding the president's "hallowed" corpse. Considering the terrible conflict that engulfed the nation beginning in 1861, and the unprecedented nature of the assassination at the end of the fighting, Northern leaders made a concerted effort to reaffirm the integrity of the Union. In a sermon the Sunday following the death, Henry Ward Beecher captured this feeling of collective urgency and danger: "The blow brought not a sharp pang. It was so terrible that at first it stunned sensibility. Citizens were like men awakened at midnight by an earthquake, and bewildered to find everything that they were accustomed to trust wavering and falling."[58]

In the second place, the most convenient and effective strategy of symbolization that could disguise and reconceptualize the violence perpetrated on Lincoln's body—as well as carried out the previous four years on battlefields throughout the country—was to turn to biblical tropes that shed light and meaning on these events. In addition to the frequent comparisons to Moses, the death and resurrection of Jesus Christ was used as a model to understand the national significance of Lincoln's murder—not surprising, considering the coincidence of the day of his assassination—and the possibility of societal redemption.

In a speech by Henry W. Bellows, Unitarian minister and president of the U.S. Sanitary Commission during the war, the parallels were unmistakable: "Meanwhile heaven rejoices this Easter morning in the resurrection of our lost leader, honored in the day of his death; dying on the anniversary of our Lord's great sacrifice, a mighty sacrifice himself for the sins of a whole people."[59] In other words, as a recent historian has argued, "Lincoln's sacrifice...made him our political Christ."[60]

In concert with these interpretations, reinforcing the links between Abraham Lincoln in death, Christianity, and national regeneration, was an equally strong reaffirmation of the power and sacrality of the state in the structure of the funeral procession in Washington, D.C., and the other cities where it was exhibited. The ceremonies enacted after he died at the White House, the long, circuitous funeral journey to Springfield, and the final disposition of the body in Oak Ridge were rituals that represented federal continuity, structure, and order. As Mary Ryan wrote about the procession in Washington, "In this moment of national sorrow, the organizers of the parade fell back on old principles of social hierarchy—at least in the front ranks of the procession, where the elite assembled in groups such as the Chamber of Commerce and the Union Club, followed immediately by state and local officials."[61]

Although there was an element of egalitarianism in the presentation and accessibility of the body during the funeral journey, it also served as a "traveling" sacred center around which the government displayed its coherence, legitimacy, and permanence. The symbolic potency of the funeral car's journey on the many miles of railroad tracks, winding its way from city to city, only enhanced the spectacle of national power emanating from the president's public body and reaffirmed the industrial superiority of Northern society.

Returning to a theme mentioned earlier, these two strategic fictions associated with Lincoln's corpse—relationship to Christ and national continuity—also recall the linguistic acrobatics explored by Ernst Kantorowicz in his examination of the legal fictions employed in the construction of the king's two bodies in England and France. In medieval funeral processions, the effigy of the king and his actual body represented two distinct images: the immortality of the crown and the transient remains of the mortal who inhabited the crown, "the triumph over Death and the triumph of Death."[62] Both images collapse and are simultaneously present in the public body of Abraham Lincoln and the activities surrounding his burial. Like the effigy, which often signified the "dignitas" or immortal nature of the kingship, the president's embalmed body was supposed to represent the immortality, the incorruptibility of the nation; the state corporealized and made flesh, bearing no marks of the violence it, and the nation, had just lived through. Just as the embalming chemicals appeared to preserve the integrity of Lincoln's corpse, the cortege winding its way through the victorious Northern states seemed to solidify the body politic as imagined by political and religious leaders. In the words of political historian Michael Rogin, "His own bleeding body bound up the nation's wounds. Carried slowly by train on a twelve-day funeral procession through the North, Lincoln's body merged with the mystic body of the Union...Lincoln helped move America from a divided, self-interested contractual association to a unified, spiritual, organic state."[63]

Besides the power of the state, there was also a domestic symbolism emanating from Lincoln's corpse. As we have seen, though, the family that appropriated this body was not the nuclear family with Mary Todd at the center, but the national family who had lost their "father" (as well as their sons) as a result of the war. This body—"hollowed" out by embalming and transported by train like other bodies during the conflict—was literally given over to the grieving relations in the Northern national community. Lincoln not only served as a father figure to those citizens who filed past the corpse, he also served as a surrogate son to those parents who lost their offspring and knew the ultimate fate of their sacrificed children (mass, anonymous burial in "profane" Southern soil). The spectacle of its presentation, less imperial than the embodiment of the national government, was based on the seemingly miraculous capacity to suspend the putrefaction and corruption of the mortal, human body and allow the living relations to behold, one last time, their lost loved one. But it must be remembered that Lincoln's body, the body that "merged with the mystic body of the Union," was in many ways an artificial body, a simulacrum of a living body at peace that disguised the instability of a vacuous, decomposing frame.

Regardless of counternarratives pointing out the apparent failure of the embalming procedure, the imagined Northern family desperately needed a memory, or memory-image, of their slain father that would evoke feelings of coherence and harmony. Although the body *did* show signs of decay and disintegration, Lincoln's deification in the collective imagination of the North required the subordination of those unpleasant, disagreeable observations calling attention to his physical body. It must be noted, though, that the discounting, and indeed the ultimate suppression, of the decomposing body in American memory represented a significant denial, a refusal to "see" and recognize the reality of death in the face of Lincoln. It also was an indication that the veneer of serenity and peace had more narrative viability than the truth lurking beneath

91

the surface. This interpretive choice was also mirrored in the larger cultural environment, where the facade of national wholeness after the war disguised persistent societal realities such as racial intolerance, regional fragmentation, and gender inequality. Throughout the 19th century, there were cultural critics and artists who noted the tendency in American life to refuse to see a deeper, more troubling reality undergirding the "New Israel."[64]

Just as there were counternarratives describing a corpse that was in decay and unpresentable, the period of mourning also produced discourses and actions that challenged the "appearance" of social solidarity in the body politic. For example, some religious leaders expressed outrage over the moral degeneration of the country and the continued oppressive conditions of African Americans; in New York, the city council refused to allow African Americans to participate in the parade at Lincoln's funeral, though some were permitted to march at the very last minute;[65] other religious as well as political leaders, as alluded to previously, advocated further violence against the South as retribution for the assassination; and, most importantly for this discussion, the first widow of a murdered president became a social outcast in her own country. The treatment and fate of Mary Todd Lincoln after her husband's death suggest that the public process of mourning and recuperation depended on severing him from his most intimate associate — his wife.

The richness of Abraham Lincoln's symbolic body is based on the erasure of his real, transient body from historical memory and especially its disconnection from the bonds of domesticity. In a culture that glorified sentimentalism and family life, the most public of families was demolished so that another might live; the excision of Mary Todd Lincoln's problematic and misunderstood living body from the reviving nation enabled the president's remains to be remembered with a different frame of reference than the normal domestic imagery employed to respond to the death of a loved one. The national work of healing did not address the condition of Mary Todd — she was excluded from this process for a number of reasons, including the severity of the mental, emotional, and physical afflictions that were believed to be rooted in her "feminine" nature,[66] and her unique status as the first woman to have a husband assassinated while in the White House. Although mention was made of her suffering in some sermons and speeches after Abraham's death, the persistent grief of Mary Todd was incompatible with the rhetorical and iconographic themes of Lincoln as "father" of the country, as providential instrument in the country's millennial destiny, and as sacrificial lamb for the redemption of the entire nation.[67]

There were other reasons for denying a symbolic link between her body and the president's deification as well. During her marriage and until the time of her own death, Mary Todd refused to be intimidated by the male-dominated world of politics. She transgressed the line separating the domestic from the political and subverted the gender rules established in 19th century America. As historian Kathryn Kish Sklar writes, "For Mary Todd Lincoln the doctrine of separate spheres did not apply. Her unladylike participation in the political arena, in the name of defending or advancing her husband's interest, earned her many enemies while she occupied the White House."[68]

After her husband's death, the mourning clothes, the fight for a pension, and the insanity trial were some of the reasons she remained in the public eye. On the other hand, what was supposed to be her special domain, the private sphere of domesticity,[69] had utterly collapsed as a result of death (of her children as well as her husband), her entrance into the political arena, and her exit from the White House. Mary Todd's desire to rehabilitate that domestic sphere by controlling the corpse — thus ensuring her own eternal relationship to it — contributed to the sense of danger she posed to the social body. In her complete devotion to her very public husband, she tried to integrate herself and the Lincoln family into the constellation of symbols erected for the sixteenth president.

Equally important to Mary Todd's absence from Northern efforts to shape the contours of national memory was the public knowledge of the widow's Southern background. This was undoubtedly a factor in her removal from the political and religious discourse that sought to transform debilitating sorrow into promise for the future. Her living presence embodied two tragic episodes in the immediate past for Northern society: the Civil War and the assassination.

In both cases, awareness of her Southern lineage opened old wounds that the collective national family had been trying to heal. Mary Todd became fixed in the collective imagination as a grim reminder of the past and the enemies who dared to inflict violence on the body politic. The representational scheme associated with her body was an inversion of everything her husband symbolized in the mythological edifice constructed around his body: she was abandoned by the North after the assassination, he was symbolically embraced as one of the critical "fathers" of the country; she was accused of being selfish, materialistic, and greedy, his life story was characterized by love of country and self-sacrifice; she was from a wealthy, Southern family, his origins were associated with poverty and a log cabin.

Mary Todd had, in effect, lost her membership in both regions of the country; she did not belong to the North or the South, and in the postwar years, as the federal government sought to enforce its rule throughout the country, her life became irrelevant to national politics. Her liminal condition in American society—resulting from her Southern heritage, constant state of mourning, mental and emotional breakdowns, public status as a widowed First Lady, etc.—did not allow her to participate in the apotheosis of her dead husband, the sixteenth president, "Father Abraham." While the kinship with the corpse expanded as the North mourned their fallen leader, sympathy for the grieving widow contracted until she too was dead.

For Mary Todd, her identity—the only identity she knew was

unalterably linked to the identity of Abraham Lincoln, but the nation had transformed the memory of her husband into a public symbol that had no room for her unstable, ambiguous presence. In addition, her private agonies reinforced her symbolic danger to the body politic—she made sense of the president's death in a way that threatened the response of Northern citizens and leaders. Even though she too spoke and wrote of her husband as a "martyr" for the country, using the very language and symbolism found in public culture to describe his sacred place in America's history, the widow would not and could not separate herself from his spirit—notions of "private" and "public" were irrelevant in her mind.

American society was stricken by Abraham Lincoln's death, but it could not let the horror of the moment detract from its destiny; instead, the body of the dead president inspired national progress and social redemption. Mary Todd Lincoln was frozen in time after the murder; her body, constantly draped in black, could not be redeemed by any symbol system—national, domestic, and religious symbols had no evocative power for citizens to give her life meaning. On a personal level, Mary Todd grew more and more incapacitated, both by her own ailments as well as the gendered language that specialists used to explain those ailments. Her physical and emotional symptoms could not be dissociated from her status as woman, mother, and widow. On a social level, Mary Todd could not live a full life because she could not reclaim her husband and bring him to the lost world of the Lincoln family; although she made her own private efforts to contact him, the federal and local governments as well as the Northern public would not allow her to be associated with the president's spirit. The only condition that would facilitate their reunion came after she died, when she too was an inanimate corpse and could be placed in the family vault.

Notes

1. Some of the biographies on Lincoln's life used in this study include Stephen B. Oates, *With Malice Toward None: The Life of Abraham Lincoln* (New York: Harper and Row, 1978); Carl Sandburg, *Abraham Lincoln: The Prairie Years and the War Years* (New York: Harcourt, Brace, 1954); and John G. Nicolay and John Hay, *Abraham Lincoln: A History* (New York: Century, 1890). For discussions that explore Lincoln in American memory, see Michael Kammen, *Mystic Chords of Memory: The Transformation of Tradition in American Culture* (New York: Alfred A. Knopf, 1991) and the more recent work that deals explicitly with Lincoln's presence in American culture, Merrill D. Peterson, *Lincoln in American Memory* (New York: Oxford University Press, 1994).

2. For a thorough discussion of demographic patterns during the Civil War, see Maris A. Vinovskis, "Have Social Historians Lost the Civil War? Some Preliminary Demographic Speculations," in *Toward a Social History of American Civil War: Exploratory Essays,* ed. Maris A. Vinovskis (Cambridge, Mass.: Cambridge University Press, 1990); also see Thomas L. Livermore, *Numbers and Losses in the Civil War in America: 1861-1865* (1900; rept., Bloomington: Indiana University Press, 1957).

3. The relationship between this corpse and changes in attitudes and practices surrounding the dead in American culture is touched upon in various books, including Richard Huntington and Peter Metcalf, *Celebrations of Death: The Anthropology of Mortuary Ritual* (Cambridge, Mass.: Cambridge University Press, 1979), 190. For a more detailed discussion, see Gary Laderman, *The Sacred Remains: American Attitudes Toward Death, 1799-1865* (New Haven, Conn., 1996).

4. The two major cultural histories dealing with these issues are Michel Vovelle, *La Mort et l'Occident: De 1300 à Nos Jours* (Paris: Gallimard, 1983); and Philippe Ariès, *The Hour of Our Death,* trans. Helen Weaver (New York: Vintage, 1981). For other studies in this area, see, for example, Robert Hertz, "A Contribution to the Study of the Collective Representations of Death," in *Death and the Right Hand,* trans. R. and C. Needham (New York: Free Press, 1960); Michel Rogin, *The Space of Death: A Study of Funerary Architecture, Decoration, and Urbanism* trans. Alan Sheridan (Charlottesville: University

Press of Virginia, 1983); Louis-Vincent Thomas, *Rites de Mort; Pour La Paix des Vivants* (Paris: Fayard, 1985); Lindsay Prior, *The Social Organization of Death: Medical Discourse and Social Practices in Belfast* (London: Macmillan, 1989); and David Chidester, *Salvation and Suicide: An Interpretation of Jim Jones, the Peoples Temple and Jonestown* (Bloomington: Indiana University Press, 1988).

5. One of the best examinations of societal responses to the death of royal figures is discussed by Huntington and Metcalf, "The Dead King," and "The Immortal Kingship," in *Celebrations of Death*. Both Vovelle and Ariès explore these issues as well.

6. There are a number of excellent studies on the subject of death that raise these issues and have assisted me in my own work on the cultural history of death, including Vovelle, *La Mort et l'Occident*; Ariès, *Hour of Our Death*; Prior, *Social Organization of Death*; Ruth Richardson, *Death, Dissection and the Destitute* (London: Penguin, 1989); and Michael C. Kearl, *Endings: A Sociology of Death and Dying* (New York: Oxford University Press, 1989).

For studies on the history of death in America see David E. Stannard, *The Puritan Way of Death: A Study in Religion, Culture, and Social Change* (Oxford: Oxford University Press, 1977); Stannard, ed., *Death in America* (Philadelphia: University of Pennsylvania Press, 1974); James J. Farrell, *Inventing the American Way of Death, 1830-1920* (Philadelphia: Temple University Press, 1980); Blanche Linden-Ward, *Silent City on a Hill: Landscapes of Memory and Boston's Mount Auburn Cemetery* (Columbus: Ohio State University Press, 1989), Robert W. Rabenstein and William M. Lamers, *The History of American Funeral Directing*, rev. ed. (Milwaukee, Wise.: Bulfin, 1962); Charles 0. Jackson, ed., *Passing: The Vision of Death in America* (Westport, Conn.: Greenwood, 1977); Lloyd W. Warner, *The Living and the Dead: A Study of the Symbolic Life of Americans* (New Haven: Yale University Press, 1959); and Laderman, *Sacred Remains*.

7. Some of the works on the life of Mary Todd Lincoln that have been particularly useful for this paper include Jean H. Baker, *Mary Todd Lincoln: A Biography* (New York: W. W. Norton, 1987); Justin G. Turner and Linda Levitt Turner, *Mary Todd Lincoln: Her Life and Letters* (New York: Alfred A. Knopf, 1972); Ruth Painter Randall, *Mary Todd Lincoln: Biography of a Marriage* (Boston: Little, Brown, 1953); and Elizabeth Keckley,

Behind the Scenes: Thirty Years a Slave and Four Years in the White House (New York: G. W. Carleton, 1868).

8. Baker, *Mary Todd Lincoln*, 134-36, 181.

9. Ibid., 181. Most biographers discuss this characteristic of Mary Todd Lincoln; also see Carl Sferrazza Anthony, *First Ladies: The Saga of the Presidents' Wives and Their Power, 1789-1961* (New York: W. Morrow, 1990), 168-200.

10. Turner and Turner, *Mary Todd Lincoln*, 77-79; Oates, *With Malice Toward None*, 297; Randall, *Mary Todd Lincoln*, 276; and Anthony, *First Ladies*, 190.

11. Baker, *Mary Todd Lincoln*, 244-45; Oates, *With Malice Toward None*, 470; and Dorothy Meserve Kunhardt and Philip B. Kunhardt, Jr., *Twenty Days: The Authoritative Account of Lincoln's Assassination, the Conspiracy, and Aftermath* (North Hollywood, Cal.: Newcastle, 1985), 39-49.

12. Baker, *Mary Todd Lincoln*, 245. Stanton is identified as the one who states this, though in a slightly different way ("Take that woman out and do not let her in again!"), in Kunhardt and Kunhardt, *Twenty Days*, 79.

13. Baker, *Mary Todd Lincoln*, 247; and Turner and Turner, *Mary Todd Lincoln*, 223.

14. Baker, *Mary Todd Lincoln*, 248; and Turner and Turner, *Mary Todd Lincoln*, 224. She expressed some of these sentiments in a letter written to Senator Charles Sumner a few months later: "My belief, is so assured, that *Death*, is only a blessed transition, to the 'pure in heart,' that a very slight veil separates us, from the 'loved & lost' and to me, there is comfort, in the thought, that though unseen by us, they are very near" (Turner and Turner, *Mary Todd Lincoln*, 256).

15. The preceding discussion was based on Kunhardt and Kunhardt, *Twenty Days*, 248-49; Randall, *Mary Todd Lincoln*, 347-48; Turner and Turner, *Mary Todd Lincoln*, 240-41; and Baker, *Mary Todd Lincoln*, 251-52. The controversy resurfaced later when Mary Todd heard that the National Lincoln Monument Association was considering a monument at the site initially proposed in the center of the city. She threatened the governor that if the monument was built there rather than in Oak Ridge, she would move her husband's body to Washington or some other eastern city that was eager for his sacred remains. When there was a suggestion that they discuss the issue, Mary Todd reiterated her intentions to control the fate of her family: "My determination is unalterable,

and...without I receive the 15th of this month a formal & written agreement that *the* Monument shall be placed over the remains of my Beloved Husband, in *Oak Ridge* Cemetery, with the *written* promise that no other bodies, save the President, his Wife, his Sons & Sons families, shall ever be deposited within the enclosure...If I had anticipated, so much trouble, in having my wishes carried out, I should have readily yielded to the request of *many* & had *his* precious remains, in the *first instance* placed in the vault of the National Capitol -A tomb prepared for Washington the Father of his Country & a fit resting place for the immortal Savior & Martyr for Freedom." (Turner and Turner, *Mary Todd Lincoln,* 243-44)

16. Keckley, *Behind the Scenes,* 208; and Turner and Turner, *Mary Todd Lincoln,* 231.

17. Baker, *Mary Todd Lincoln,* 253; and James M. McPherson, *Battle Cry of Freedom: The Civil War Era* (New York: Ballantine, 1988), 853.

18. See Baker, *Mary Todd Lincoln,* 275; Turner and Turner, *Mary Todd Lincoln,* 431-32; and Randall, *Mary Todd Lincoln,* 367-79.

19. A book she enjoyed reading while in Europe was Elizabeth Stuart Phelp's *The Gates Ajar* (Boston: Fields, Osgood, 1868), one of the most popular books to come out after the Civil War. As Ann Douglas points out, this book—whose main character is named Mary, a woman devastated by the death of her brother during the war—epitomizes much of the consolation literature of the period, grounding heaven in a material, domestic realm, yet affirming the close, spiritual presence of those who have passed on (Douglas, *The Feminization of American Culture* [New York: Alfred A. Knopf, 1977], 269-70).

20. Turner and Turner, *Mary Todd Lincoln,* 474-75; also see the discussion in Baker, *Mary Todd Lincoln,* 269-70.

21. Baker, *Mary Todd Lincoln,* 281-306. Her response to the gossip about her marriage plans can be found in a letter to Sally Orne in Turner and Turner, *Mary Todd Lincoln,* 537.

22. Baker, *Mary Todd Lincoln,* 295-302. Mary Todd's letters acknowledge the cruel treatment she received in the press. See, for example, Turner and Turner, *Mary Todd Lincoln,* 529.

23. Turner and Turner, *Mary Todd Lincoln,* 597-98.

24. On the imagery that brought Washington and Lincoln together, see Marcus Cunliffe, *The Doubled Images of Lincoln and Washington* (Gettysburg, Pa.: Gettysburg College, 1988). A brief description of Field's painting is found in Abraham A. Davidson, *The Eccentrics and Other American Visionary Painters* (New York: Dutton, 1978), 89.

25. "Mrs. Abraham Lincoln, Trial of the Question of Her Sanity in Chicago: A Verdict That She Is Insane Is Rendered," *New York Times*, May 20, 1987, 2; also see the discussion in Baker, *Mary Todd Lincoln*, 319-20.

26. Baker, *Mary Todd Lincoln*, 319-20.

27. Quoted in Baker, *Mary Todd Lincoln*, 321; also see Mark E. Neely, Jr., and R. Gerald McMurty, *The Insanity File: The Case of Mary Todd Lincoln* (Carbondale: Southern Illinois University Press, 1986), 6-17.

28. *New York Times*, 2.

29. For further discussions about this episode in Mary Todd's life, see Turner and Turner, *Mary Todd Lincoln*, 608-14; Baker, *Mary Todd Lincoln*, 315-50; and Neely and McMurtry, *Insanity File*.

30. Baker, *Mary Todd Lincoln*, 368.

31. Turner and Turner, *Mary Todd Lincoln*, 717.

32. Ishbel Ross, *The President's Wife, Mary Todd Lincoln: A Biography* (New York: G. P. Putnam's Sons, 1973), 333-34; Turner and Turner, *Mary Todd Lincoln*, 716-17; and Baker, *Mary Todd Lincoln*, 368-69.

33. David B. Chesebrough, *"No Sorrow Like Our Sorrow": Northern Protestant Ministers and the Assassination of Lincoln* (Kent, Ohio: Kent State University Press, 1994), 53-65.

34. For a brief discussion of the reaction to Lincoln's death in the South, see Michael Davis, *The Image of Lincoln in the South* (Knoxville: University of Tennessee Press, 1971), 98-104; and Thomas Reed Turner, *Beware the People Weeping: Public Opinion and the Assassination of Abraham Lincoln* (Baton Rouge: Louisiana State University Press, 1982), 90-99.

35. "Particulars of the Killing of Lincoln and Seward," Augusta, Ga., *Daily Constitutionalist*, April 23, 1865, 2.

36. Kunhardt and Kunhardt, *Twenty Days*, 1.

37. Quoted in ibid., 80.

38. My own research on cultural attitudes toward death and the dead addresses many of these shifting patterns in American culture (see Laderman, *Sacred Remains).*

39. Kunhardt and Kunhardt, *Twenty Days,* 93.

40. Ibid., 95; also see John Gilmary Shea, ed., *The Lincoln Memorial: A Record of the Life, Assassination, and Obsequies of the Martyred President,* (New York: Bunce and Huntington, 1865), 111.

41. "Treatment of the President's Body," Pittsburgh *Daily Post,* April 22, 1865, 1.

42. Kunhardt and Kunhardt, *Twenty Days,* 120; and Sandburg, *Abraham Lincoln,* 735.

43. For one account of many of the activities around the country, see Shea, *Lincoln Memorial.*

44. "The Appearance of the Corpse," Philadelphia *Daily Evening Bulletin,* April 24, 1865, 2.

45. Charles A. Page, *Letters from a War Correspondent,* ed. James R. Gilmore (Boston: L. L. Page, 1899), 364.

46. "Appearance of the Body," *Indianapolis Daily Journal,* May 2, 1865, 2.

47. "Account of the Presidents Funeral Train," *New York Times,* April 25, 1865, 2; also see remarks in Sandburg, *Abraham Lincoln,* 739.

48. "Report on Body and Funeral," *Cleveland Daily Plain Dealer,* April 26, 1865, 2.

49. Ellen Kean, *Death and Funeral of Abraham Lincoln: A Contemporary Description by Mrs. Ellen Kean* (London, privately printed, 1921), 22. (Illinois State Historical Library, Springfield, Ill.).

50. Kunhardt and Kunhardt, *Twenty Days,* 256.

51. Ibid., 256-57.

52. George Bancroft, "How Shall the Nation Show Its Sorrow?" in *Building the Myth: Selected Speeches Memorializing Abraham Lincoln,* ed. Waldo W. Braden (Urbana: University of Illinois Press, 1990), 71.

53. Shea, *Lincoln Memorial,* 230-31.

54. Ibid., 231. For a recent analysis of the religious discourse that appeared in the North after the assassination, see Chesebrough, *"No Sorrow."*

55. Sidney E. Mead, *The Lively Experiment: The Shaping of Christianity in America* (New York: Harper and Row, 1963), 73.

56. In their discussion of the dead king, anthropologists Huntington and Metcalf write that "royal death rites are special because they are part of a political drama in which many people have a stake. Especially in kingdoms in which the state is personified by the monarch, the king's funeral was an event that reverberated with far-reaching political and even cosmological implications" *(Celebrations of Death,* 122). They also briefly discuss the significance of Lincoln's death in the conclusion of their book.

57. Others who have written on Lincoln's symbolism in death include Robert Bellah, "Civil Religion in America," in *Beyond Belief: Essays in Religion in Post Traditional World* (New York: Harper and Row, 1970), 168-89; Michael Rogin, "The King's Two Bodies: Lincoln, Wilson, Nixon, and Presidential Self-Sacrifice," in *Ronald Reagan, the Movie, and Other Episodes in Political Demonology* (Berkeley: University of California Press, 1987); and Huntington and Metcalf, *Celebrations of Death,* 206.

58. Shea, *Lincoln Memorial,* 103.

59. Ibid., 98.

60. Rogin, "King's Two Bodies," 83.

61. Mary Ryan, "The American Parade: Representations of the Nineteenth Century Social Order," in *The New Cultural History,* ed. Lynn Hunt (Berkeley: University of California Press, 1989), 143.

62. Ernst H. Kantorowicz, *The King's Two Bodies: A Study in Medieval Political Theology* (Princeton: Princeton University Press, 1957), 429.

63. Rogin, "King's Two Bodies," 90.

64. For a recent analysis of this predisposition in 19th-century literature, see David S. Reynolds, *Beneath the American Renaissance: The Subversive Imagination in the Age of Emerson and Melville* (Cambridge, Mass: Alfred A. Knopf, 1989).

65. Kunhardt and Kunhardt, *Twenty Days,* 153.

66. The association of her afflictions with feminine characteristics was a common medical diagnosis in the gendered rhetoric of sickness and disease in the period. For one of the best analyses of these issues, see Barbara Ehrenreich and Deirdre English, *For Her Own Good: 150 Years of the Experts' Advice to Women* (New York: Anchor, 1979).

On gender and mourning, see Karen Halttunen, *Confidence Men and Painted Women: A Study of Middle-Class Culture in America, 1830-1870* (New Haven: Yale University Press, 1982).

67. As so many people who have heard or read this paper have remarked, the parallels and differences with the experience of Jackie Onasis Kennedy in the mid-20th century are worth exploring. Her life and recent death, as well as the passing of Richard Nixon, are contemporary case studies that continue to illustrate the relationship between the deaths of national figures and the necessary work of defining and redefining the meaning of America.

68. Kathryn Kish Sklar, "Victorian Women and Domestic Life: Mary Todd Lincoln, Elizabeth Cady Stanton, and Harriet Beecher Stowe," in *Women and Power in American History: A Reader, Vol.I to 1880,* ed. Kathryn Kish Sklar and Thomas Dublin (Englewood Cliffs, N.J.: Prentice Hall, 1991), 240.

69. On the history of women and the domestic sphere in American life, see, for example, Barbara Welter, *Dimity Convictions: The American Woman in the Nineteenth Century* (Athens: Ohio University Press, 1976); Nancy F. Cott, *The Bonds of Womanhood: "Woman's Sphere" in New England, 1780-1835* (New Haven: Yale University Press, 1977); Catherine Clinton, *The Other Civil War: American Women in the Nineteenth Century* (New York: Hill and Wang, 1984); and Carroll Smith-Rosenberg, *Disorderly Conduct: Visions of Gender in Victorian America* (New York: Oxford University Press, 1985).

Published with permission from Cambridge University Press. Laderman, G. (1997). The Body Politic and the Politics of Two Bodies: Abraham and Mary Todd Lincoln in Death. Prospects, 22, 109-132 © Cambridge University Press 1997

2.

The Disney Way of Death

The man most intimately associated with the imagination of children in twentieth-century America is Walt Disney. His lasting cultural power is a testament to his creative energies, bold innovations, philosophy of entertainment, and identification with dominant American values; the fact that his work continues to shape the fantasy life of generations of children only makes his crucial position in American cultural history more obvious. Disney's life, beginning in Chicago at the turn of the century and ending in a hospital directly across the street from his Burbank studios in 1966, is a paradigmatic American rags-to-riches story. But his achievements were not solely limited to success in the business of entertainment.

Disney's cultural productions, including films, television shows, and theme parks, have left an indelible mark on the life of the nation. In many ways, his work helped usher in the emerging value systems that transformed the United States in the first part of the century. According to recent biographer Steven Watts, "In the broadest sense, Disney smoothed the jagged transition from the values of the Victorian age to those of the fledgling consumer America...[H]e helped Americans

105

accommodate to a new age by appealing to older traditions while forging a new creed of leisure, self-fulfillment, and mass consumption. More than a mere cartoonist or entertainer, he managed to become, to use his own phrase, a spokesman for the American way of life" (163). Taken as a whole, the mythic worlds animated and brought to life in Disney's work provide Americans with both an escape from reality and effective interpretive tools to make sense of reality—in other words, his cultural legacy has as much to do with religion as it does with mass entertainment.

It Disney was a mouthpiece for an American way of life, the force of his voice depended on a curious obsession with death—not surprising considering the usual connections between the religious imagination and mortality (see, for example, Sullivan). While recent critical studies have begun to examine the rich cultural material found in his life and work, focusing on gender, sexuality, class, and politics, little has been said about a glaring propensity to focus on death in many of his early films (Bryman; Bell, Haas, and Sells; Willis). The following essay will address this lacuna and investigate Disney's cultural productions in relation to cultural history, American religious life, and a burgeoning field of study, the history of death.

DEATH IN AMERICA: TABOO OR NOT TABOO?

Conventional wisdom holds that America is a death-denying culture. From the early 1960s psychologists, sociologists, nurses, doctors, anthropologists, historians, journalists, and others have supported this cultural diagnosis, which has proven to be a powerful trope in the literature on death in America. Relying in part on the assumption that there is a universal fear of death, many writers have argued that the subject of death in American society is taboo, that the reality of death has disappeared from everyday life, that death itself has become bereft of meaning for most people—particularly over the course of the first half of the twentieth century.

An explosion of writings on death began to appear by the end of the 1960s, and the argument about an "age of death denial" has carried the day since. Those early studies shaped conventional wisdom about the past and convinced a nation that its views on death were determined by out-of-control modernizing social forces, irrational personal anxieties, and culturally pervasive taboos. In the preface to *The Meaning of Death* (1959), one of the first publications to address this topic, Herman Feifel makes an important observation about death in America: it has not attracted much scholarly attention.

He writes, "Even after looking hard in the literature, it is surprising how slim is the systematized knowledge about death. Far too little heed has been given to assessing thoroughly the implications of the meaning of death" (v). Feifel, a psychologist who served as editor for this collection of essays, rightly recognizes the unique status of the book, both as a contribution to the interdisciplinary study of death and as a premier text in a new field of research in America.

Before explaining the organization of the book, which includes sections on theory, psychology, and sociology, Feifel makes the following cultural observation: "In the presence of death, Western culture, by and large, has tended to run, hide, and seek refuge in group norms and actuarial statistics. The individual face of death has become blurred by embarrassed incuriosity [sic] and institutionalization. The shadows have begun to dwarf the substance. Concern about death has been relegated to the tabooed territory heretofore occupied by diseases like tuberculosis and cancer and the topic of sex. We have been compelled, in unhealthy measure, to internalize our thoughts and feelings, fears, and even hopes concerning death" (xii).

Although Feifel refers to "Western culture" in this passage, he is primarily concerned about American society, as he makes clear when he identifies the first "dominant leitmotif" running throughout the book: "Denial and avoidance of the countenance of death characterize much of the American outlook" (xv).

Similar observations had been made before Feifel's, but in many respects this collection marks a turning point in the published literature on death in America. The principal characteristics associated with the American experience of death—invisibility, silence, dispassion, institutionalization, taboo—can be found in almost every subsequent publication on the topic.

As suggested earlier, the proliferation of literature on death in America was produced by people associated with a number of social settings, including universities, hospitals, therapy sessions, hospices, and funeral homes. Although the focus of these writings varied, most either implicitly maintained or actively supported the notion that America was a death denying culture. One of the most authoritative voices to shape public opinion was Elizabeth Kübler-Ross, whose *On Death and Dying* (1969) popularly linked the vocabulary of denial with the language of death.

Kübler-Ross identified denial as the first stage to the ultimate acceptance of death among terminal patients, but she also argued for a much larger social tendency to refuse the reality of death. Kübler-Ross first describes a childhood experience with death she had growing up in Europe that was distinguished by acceptance, communal support, and mature realism. She then states how this compares with America at mid-century: "This is in great contrast to a society in which death is viewed as taboo, discussion of it is regarded as morbid, and children are excluded with the presumption and pretext that it would be 'too much' for them" (6-7).

Important features of the literature on death are the lack of attention to religion and the often tacit assumption that the forces of secularization were demystifying the realities of death and expunging them from everyday life. The modern experience of death, as it appears in much of the literature, was generally linked to such recent social developments as the rise of hospitals as places of dying, advancements in scientific and medical knowledge, increased analytic interest in the psychology of grief, and the dramatic economic growth of funeral homes throughout the country. The passage from life to death, and the physical remains after the last breath, became associated with a range of secular values and technological interventions rather than traditional spiritual questions and theological explanations.

In the introduction to a collection of primarily social scientific studies of death published in 1965, Robert Fulton employs imagery from the field of medicine to characterize the shift from a religious to a secular perspective on death overtaking contemporary culture: "In America today we have come to a point in our history when we are beginning to react to death as we would to a communicable disease. Death no longer is viewed as the price of moral trespass or as the result of theological wrath; rather, in our modern secular world, death is coming to be seen as the consequence of personal neglect or untoward accident. Death is now a temporal matter. Like cancer or syphilis, it is a private disaster that we discuss only reluctantly with our physician. Moreover, as in the manner of many contagious diseases, those who are caught in the throes of death are isolated from their fellow human beings, while those who have succumbed to it are hidden quickly from view" (Fulton: 4).

For many writing on the subject in the 1960s, 1970s, and 1980s, the invisibility of death in American culture was produced in an increasingly secular society—in other words, arguments about the disappearance of death went hand-in-hand with arguments about the "desacralization" of death.

One of the most important figures to perpetuate the notion that, in his words, "society has banished death," is French historian, Philippe Ariès. His monumental study of attitudes toward death in western society, *The Hour of Our Death*, concludes with an analysis of the twentieth century, tellingly labeled "The Invisible Death."

In the chapter, "Death Denied," Ariès turns to a discussion of the United States. Rather than push the denial thesis full force, he presents a much more subtle commentary on the contradictory cultural forces at work in the first half of the twentieth century. On the one hand, he writes, "it is as if one whole part of the culture were pushing America to erase every vestige of death…It is the [trend] that is spreading the taboo about death or the idea of the insignificance of death throughout the modern world."

On the other hand, Ariès understands the American funeral as a site where a contradictory attitude toward death finds expression, a place where death remains "quite visible" and firmly in the mind of the living (596).

While Ariès is one of the few to suggest that America has more complicated views on death than previously believed, the first trend, related to erasures and taboos, is the one most often reaffirmed by those who refer to his work. It is also the prevailing view found in another relevant source of information: textbooks on death and dying, a growth industry by the end of the 1970s. In a recent example from *Confronting Death: Values, Institutions, and Human Mortality* (1996) David Wendell Moller presents an historical overview of attitudes toward death based on Ariès's research on the European context. He then moves "across the ocean" to America and, although briefly commenting on death in Puritan New England and nineteenth-century society, focuses on "the disappearance of death" in the twentieth century. Like Ariès, Moller quickly raises the possibility that American attitudes might be more nuanced and complicated than they appear. But he, like so many others, concludes this discussion by falling back on conventional wisdom and historical nostalgia for a bygone era: "The traditional orientation to death with its essential patterns of religion, ritual, and community, has been replaced by the denial, confusion, contradiction, and meaninglessness of the modern styles of death and dying" (13-14; quote from 22).

Although the weight of these arguments is strong, they either do not tell the whole story about death in American society or only hint at the possibility that American responses do not have to be classified as forms of denial or acceptance. Instead of readily accepting the sweeping generalizations associated with the "taboo" argument, a more intricate cultural analysis must take into account the simultaneous presence of prohibitions and public expressions and make sense of the variety of responses to death—often distinctly religious responses—that can be found circulating within American society. The material and cultural landscape is too infested with ghosts, personal lives too haunted by the loss of significant others, collective memory too dependent on the blood of martyrs and victims, for death to easily slip away from the sight of living Americans—even in the first half of the twentieth century.

In addition to the silence and whispers surrounding death during this period of time there were telling signs of preoccupation with the end of life and fascination with the unmistakable realities of death. Numerous case studies from the twentieth-century could be explored, including the rise of successful funeral homes across the country, the impact of two world wars on American sensibilities, the growing literature in the psychology of grief, and the variety of representations of death found in popular culture.

The rest of this essay will explore a series of popular representations of death in American culture that can be found in films produced by Walt Disney during his life. These texts offer evidence of a set of cultural meanings different from those associated with the taboo arguments. In order to understand these meanings better, it will be necessary to stray from the texts themselves and consider both the audience which flocked to the films and the man who produced them.

Gary Laderman

"DEATH, DISNEY'S OBSESSION WITH"

Walt Disney is a complex American figure, and the picture that has emerged in numerous studies of his life contains telling contradictions. A creator of beloved cartoon characters like Jimminy Cricket, Bambi, and Dopey, but also an anti-Semite who saw Jewish conspiracy and corruption all around him; a patriotic American who made propaganda films for the U.S. military in World War II, and an FBI informant who ratted on other early Hollywood pioneers; an industrious, self-made man who stands as an icon for ingenuity and creativity, yet for many an industrial tyrant who exploited the labor of others. As suggested earlier, Walt Disney the man is just as attractive to the cultural historian as "Uncle Walt," one of the most significant myth-makers in twentieth-century America.

Rather than begin with the usual celebration of Walt Disney's imaginative and profoundly popular animated films, let us turn to a little discussed cruel act of brutality that one writer places at the center of his success. Biographical information about Walt Disney has been a well-guarded secret by the Disney corporation until recently, but this illuminating early life experience was reported in a 1938 edition of *The New York Times Magazine*.

In the article—one of the few written with Disney's cooperation—Douglas Churchill suggests that Disney's philosophy about entertainment can be tied to a specific experience of death in childhood:

An owl drowning in the cool shade of a tree on a Missouri farm one afternoon thirty years ago influenced the career of a man and helped fashion the fantasy of an era. Blinking in the uncomfortable light, the bird felt hands encircling it. Instinctively it beat its wings and clawed, and just as instinctively a frightened lad of 7 hurled the owl to the ground and, in his terror, stomped on it.

That owl is the only thing that Walt Disney ever intentionally killed. The incident has haunted him over the years. Occurring in a formative period, it directed his attention, subconsciously, to the birds and gentle beasts that play such an important part in his craftsmanship, and helped to shape his philoso- phy. (9)

According to a later biographer, Disney felt such stinging remorse afterward that he decided to bury the dead owl. But even though the owl had been put in the ground, it apparently haunted the dreams of the young boy for some time (Thomas: 28).

Roughly ten years prior to Churchill's 1938 article, Disney produced the first of the Silly Symphonies, an animated short called "The Skeleton Dance" (1929), which contained haunting, though hilarious, images of death. It was released just before the stock market crash in October and on the heels of Disney's enormously popular short, "Steamboat Willie," which introduced the world to Micky Mouse (Jackson: 18). The idea of animating skeletons in a graveyard to perform a modern, and playful, dance of death appealed to Disney, who began working on the cartoon with his early associate, Ubbe Iwerks. The final product depicts four skel- etons dancing in a moonlit graveyard to a musical composition derived from Edvard Grieg's, "March of the Dwarfs" (Watts: 38).

Originally titling the piece "The Spook Dance," Disney expressed his enthusiasm for its commercial prospects in a letter to Iwerks: "I am glad the spook dance is progressing so nicely—give her Hell, Ubbe—make it funny and I am sure we will be able to place it in a good way" (Thomas: 99). He also wrote to his wife, Lilly, that he was convinced of its suc- cess: "I feel positive the 'Spook Dance' will make a real hit when shown" (Thomas: 99).

Contrary to a deep-rooted American tradition of popular death im- agery in which the afterlife is depicted with domesticated scenes of pious family members reunited in the great beyond, this modern dance maca- bre relies on the physical return of the dead literally to get in the face of the living—in one sequence, the dancing skeleton's face moves forward and fills the entire frame of the screen (Douglas; McDannell and Lang). Initially, all the theater managers who previewed it hated the macabre piece, with one purportedly exclaiming to Walt's brother, Roy, "What's he trying to do, ruin us? You go back and tell that brother of yours the renters don't want this gruesome crap ... What they want is more Mickey Mouse. You go back and tell Walt. More mice, tell him, More mice!" (Mosley: 123; also see Thomas: 100).

According to another account, one exhibitor "visibly shivered after he had seen it and said it would give his customers goose bumps" (Mosley: 124). While many were shocked by Disney's thematic choice, the first Silly Symphony finally had a showing in Los Angeles, where critics and patrons raved about it, turning the "gruesome crap" into the national hit Disney expected (Thomas: 100). Two years after the Churchill piece, Disney released *Fantasia* (1940), a full-length feature film that consisted of animated stories and images set to seven classical pieces of music. It was a highly experimental film, and, although critics disagreed on its merits, the public response was clear: it was Disney's first major box office flop (although in time, it too became a money-making project for Disney) (Watts: 113-119).

The final sequence of this series of short segments actually contains two very different pieces: Mussorgsky's "Night on Bald Mountain" and Schubert's "Ava Maria." As a rather simplistic meditation on the battle between good and evil, the entire sequence moves literally from the darkness and destruction of night to the glory and beauty of the rising sun. In spite of the uplifting, spiritually inspiring scenes set to the Schubert piece, the imagery associated with "Night on Bald Mountain" is particularly graphic for a Disney film.

The sequence returns the audience to the space of a haunted graveyard, though this time the mood is less lighthearted and the setting is much more menacing to the living. In this version, the dance of death is a decidedly adult affair, with fantastic visions of monstrous demons, dangerous witches, and a mountain top transformed into an evil overlord who controls the spirits of death in the tiny village cemetery below. The sexual and highly sadistic energy that animates this segment arises from a curious mixture of images, including resurrection of the dead, transformative fires from hell, and the seductive lure of malevolent femininity and female body parts. Fortunately for the living, just as the demonic forces are about to invade the village next to the burial ground, daylight strikes and the church bells begin to toll. At this point the music shifts to Schubert, and a fog-shrouded line of candle-carrying pilgrims emerges on the screen, and daylight overtakes the night.

Disney's fascination with the dance of death, his early childhood experience, and, as we will see, the recurring death-related themes in his films all lead to a question that the title of this section answers: did Disney have an obsession with death? Richard Schickel's biography, *The Disney Vision: The Life, Times, Art and Commerce of Walt Disney* (1968), contains the index entry: "Death, Disney's obsession with" (440).

Schickel and other biographers, including Disney's own daughter, Diane, include this personality trait in their reconstruction of Disney's life. Although the Disney corporation tried to keep the personal life of the founder out of the public eye — according to Schickel, because "corporate drive has always been toward the preservation of an easily assimilated image" (11) — this characteristic and other revealing aspects of Disney's personality that have come to light in recent studies provide a more complete picture of the man than the "image" originally managed by his family and the studio.

The first to suggest that Disney was obsessed with death was his daughter, whose account of its origins is a standard feature in the prevailing Disney lore. According to Diane, in the early 1930s Disney attended a Hollywood party and had an unfortunate session with a fortune teller, who gave him some particularly bad news: he would die at thirty-five. At this point in his life, Disney had achieved enormous financial success and become a bona-fide celebrity; but, in the words of Schickel, this prediction "plagued" Disney, and "For the rest of his life he avoided funerals and when forced to attend them, fell into long, brooding depressions. He even avoided would be biographers, commenting to more than one acquaintance that 'biographies are only written about dead people'" (146).

Other biographies note that this prediction remained with Disney into his later years. Leonard Mosley writes that at a party celebrating his thirtieth wedding anniversary, Disney had been drinking quite a bit and at one point "gloomily speculated out loud whether the fortune-teller might have made a mistake. Could she have meant he was going to die at fifty-five and not thirty-five — next year, in fact?" (253).

While the psychological effects of this preoccupation are numerous, at least one biographer suggests that Disney was "in a race against time" to finish all of his projects (Thomas: 225). One of the projects he did not see to fruition but was passionate about near the end of his life, was the creation of a futuristic city, what he described as an "experimental prototype community of tomorrow"— EPCOT. According to Mosley, this vision of a tightly-controlled, highly regulated utopic community can also be linked to another expression of Disney's obsession with death: his curiosity about cryogenics, a technologically-innovative form of real-life "suspended animation." Cryogenics attracted a great deal of attention in the 1960s as a sophisticated scientific intervention in the dying process — in effect freezing the corpse until a future date, when advances in medical science could allow for the reanimation of life. Mosley argues that in Disney's mind EPCOT had profound implications for the future of humanity and links his enthusiasm for the project to his newfound interest: "Faced by mankind's suicidal impulse to destroy itself by nuclear war or the poison of pollution from toxic wastes, Walt Disney had envisaged EPCOT as the community of the future from which all the blights and blemishes of twentieth-century civilization had been banished. It would demonstrate that if people would only learn how to live in an enlightened and sanitized environment, they would be able to avoid not just war and disease but indefinitely postpone death and enjoy life, health, and happiness almost everlasting...It was about this time [early 1960s] that Walt Disney became acquainted with the experiments into the process known as cryogenesis" (287-288).

While some question the truth of Disney's interest in this scientific chimera, it too has found a permanent place in Disney lore. When Disney died of acute circulatory collapse on December 15, 1966, the studio delayed making an announcement for one day for a variety of reasons, including a concern about the financial impact of the news. According to family members who attended a private ceremony, between the death and the public notification Disney was cremated and deposited in Forest Lawn Cemetery in Los Angeles. Despite this official version of events, rumors that Disney's body had been frozen and secretly stored in an undisclosed location began to circulate almost immediately in popular consciousness.

Watts discounts such a "wild rumor," writing that "Walt's supposed interest in cryogenesis prompted speculation that his body had been frozen and stored in a lab somewhere to be revived later. There was no truth to this story" (447). The cultural durability of this "speculation" continues to be strong, however; one of the many persistent rumors about Disney's deep-freeze is that he was cryogenically sealed and placed within the confines of Cinderella's palace.

Another source for evidence of Disney's obsession with death can be found in the stories he depicted in full-length feature animated films, films that left a lasting impression on American culture in general and generations of children in particular. Indeed, the popularity of his films as both mass entertainment and socially significant pedagogical texts in the moral development of children suggests that an investigation of the role and symbolism of death in the films themselves can lead to greater understanding of the larger cultural and religious meanings associated with his work. In this light, films that gave expression to Disney's obsessions and became defining narratives in American mythology provide important material for the examination of twentieth-century society.

FEARS, FAIRY TALES, AND AMERICAN CULTURAL RELIGION

According to many studies, Disney was both pioneer and prophet in American society. For historians, biographers, and cultural critics, his work articulated a range of celebrated American doctrines in a form that any child could understand. The success of his cultural productions mark Disney as a formidable presence in the making of modern culture. In many biographies, the story of his life is the story of twentieth-century America herself. Disney's genius lay in the ability to both express the popular sentiments and values of "the people" and reinforce particular conservative social tendencies in response to the political, economic, and cultural changes of the period. According to Watts, Disney the man and Disney the corporation grasped essential American views about social order, particularly as they relate to work and family, during an era of tremendous historical change. "In a stream of memorable work over several generations, he shaped into a synthetic, compelling form the diverse bundle of images, values, and sensibilities that many twentieth-century Americans struggled with—individualism and community, fantasy and technology, populism and corporate authority, modernism and sentimentalism, consumerism and producerism, progress and nostalgia" (452).

Watts rightly notes the distressing tendencies that emerged in both Disney's life and American society in the early twentieth century—a drift toward authoritarianism, dependence on social conformity, and deep rooted anti-intellectualism, to name a few. But he also acknowledges an unmistakable popular sentiment that remains to this day: "in typical 'American Century' style, [Disney] expressed a mythical, idealized

version of the values and aspirations of the modern United States" (453). His films are especially significant cultural productions; they act, in fact, as modern fairy tales, primarily but not exclusively created for the consumption of children, and convey distinctive religious messages about life and meaning in the twentieth century. These messages can be characterized as "religious" because they teach about order, meaning, transcendence, and orientation. In addition, like many religious expressions, they acquire social weight because they are so intimately tied to a desire to triumph over death, a point to be discussed shortly.

The audience for Disney's films, as for most fairy tales, includes adults as well as children — indeed, the timeless quality of these stories partially depends on their attracting people from every age. But the association of fairy tales with children, and the assumption that they are integral to the socialization and development of children are recent phenomena. As literary critic Maria Tatar argues in her study of the Grimms' fairy tales: "Originally told at fireside gatherings or in spinning circles by adults to adult audiences, fairy tales joined the canon of children's literature... only in the last two or three centuries. Yet the hold these stories have on the imagination of children is so compelling that it becomes difficult to conceive of a childhood without them" (xiv).

She also makes the important observation that, while fairy tales express "our deepest hopes and most ardent desires," they also contain within them darker visions: "Wishes and fantasies may come to life in the fairy tale, but fears and phobias also become full-blooded presences" (xv). The fact that the Grimms' tales include instances of "murder, mutilation, cannibalism, infanticide, and incest" makes Tatars arguments even more convincing on this point (3).

Although many understand fairy tales as tapping into universal structures and predispositions in the human psyche, some cultural historians strive to keep these stories in perspective — that is, they explore the social context in which certain stories appear and thrive, and they

119

chart how these stories change over time (Tatar: xiii-xx). For cultural historian Robert Darnton, such stories "are historical documents. They have evolved over many centuries and have taken different turns in different cultural traditions. Far from expressing the unchanging operations of man's inner being, they suggest that mentalities themselves have changed" (13).

Some of Disney's films are entirely modern, but many are drawn from the deep well of European folklore (e.g., *Snow White and the Seven Dwarfs* [1937], *Cinderella* [1950], and *Sleeping Beauty* [1959]). Darnton and others argue that the content, tenor, and texture of these tales depend on historical period and national setting.

Regardless of origin and their timeless nature, Disney tales reflect twentieth-century American society and dominant American mentalities, or worldviews. They also express certain religious sensibilities on the American landscape that are not contained within the bounds of any particular religious tradition. The study of American religion outside the boundaries of specific traditions—that is, with an anthropological eye squarely on cultural forms of expression and behavior—is a relatively new area of investigation that challenges long-held assumptions about what counts as data. Whether religion is paired with "civil," "popular culture," or "vernacular," Americanists have slowly begun to realize there is more to religious history than denominations, doctrines, and deliverance (Bellah; Chidester; McDannell; Primiano).

Historian of religions Catherine Albanese identifies one form of this religion as "American cultural religion" and argues that, though "diffuse and loose," it can be understood as an integral component of American religious history. According to Albanese, American cultural religion is a complex, multilayered religious system, providing people with "additional symbolic centers" that contain distinctive themes, practices, meanings, and value orientations that upset the conventional boundaries between the ordinary and the extraordinary. Along with two other symbolic

centers in society that promote identification with core American values, civil religion and public Protestantism, cultural religion "seeks to dissolve differences in American life" (499). Some of the pervasive themes found within it include millennial dominance and millennial innocence, the search for "religious experience and for a community of feeling," the redemptive nature of some forms of violence, perfectionism, and commitment to personal fulfillment.

Another book that explores this kind of religious sensibility in America, *The American Monomyth*, devotes an entire chapter to Disney. The authors, Robert Jewett and John Lawrence, argue that a particularly powerful mythic structure inhabits the American imagination and that one of its dominant tropes is the saving, redemptive actions of one individual in the face of dangerous evil. They examine a range of materials within American popular culture to investigate the "ritually predictable plots in the mythic landscape [that] provide some of the best clues to tensions and hopes within current American consciousness" (xi).

Jewett and Lawrence highlight the ways in which this monomyth represents a peculiar form of popular religion and suggest that Disney himself "credibly reinstated the sense of the miraculous" with his cultural productions (141). They also emphasize the acknowledged pedagogic force of his "entertainment": "Disney's efforts to create a sanitary form of happiness were regarded as the finest examples of educational entertainment" (140). The "sanitary form of happiness" that shines through by the end of the narratives depends, in fact, on the triumph over death.

In his stories, the Disney way of death is structured around "ritually predictable plots"—indeed, in addition to articulating crucial aspects of American cultural religion, his films provide Americans young and old alike with templates for understanding death. The presence of death in his films is so significant in this regard because these representations convey moral teachings about so many of the essentials of life, including sex, kinship, transcendence, suffering, and misfortune. During a period that witnessed severe economic turmoil, a second world war, scientific and technological revolutions, and other tumultuous social developments in the 1930s, 1940s, and 1950s, Disney's early animated films simultaneously entertained the masses and inculcated Americans with simplistic notions of right and wrong, virtue and vice, and innocence and corruption. And what is most striking—though not surprising—about these films is that for many stories, death, or the threat of death, is the motor, the driving force that enlivens each narrative. In addition, the preoccupation with the individual encounter with death, the impact of death on family members, and the optimistic view that death can be overcome found in most of these films, offered Americans in the first half of the twentieth century an accessible, generally Christian and broadly American, religious vision that avoided fundamentalist, apocalyptic scenarios, on the one hand, and abstruse, theological reflection, on the other (Boyer; McDannell and Lang: 326-332).

The pivotal role of death in these stories is unmistakable: in *Snow White and the Seven Dwarfs* (1937) the queen's desire to kill the young girl sets the story in motion; in *Pinocchio* (1940) the wooden puppet has to die in order to be resurrected as a real boy; in *Bambi* (1942) the small fawn becomes a mature deer in the aftermath of his mother's cruel murder; the *Cinderella* (1950) story begins with the death of her mother, which in turn leads to the introduction of the step-family; and in *Sleeping Beauty* (1959) the mortal curse by the evil fairy, Maleficent, leads the three good fairies to hide the princess in the woods. Rather than disappearing from sight, death and death-related themes are front and center in these films. Contrary to arguments about denial, these animated cartoons—like many fairy tales and other forms of children literature (Pyles; Tatar)—demonstrate a fixation on the presence of death in life.

One of the only people to discuss this characteristic in Disney films was an educational psychologist who wrote a piece for the English journal *New Society*. After the re-release of *Fantasia* (1940) in London in 1968,

Nicholas Tucker states in his essay, "Who's Afraid of Walt Disney?": "With his penchant for melodramatic settings, and his preoccupation with grief, death and bereavement, Disney is curiously old-fashioned. In some ways he anticipated the 1950 boom in horror comics, which also tended to have a 19th century air of morbidity about them. Death or near-death abounds" (502). Tucker is correct to insert this morbidity into a much larger history; indeed, in the American context this persistent fascination with death, and its representational weight in popular culture, must be understood as a critical dimension of American cultural religion.

It is often, though not always the case, that in Disney films the threat of death is framed in millennial terms—that is, powerful forces in the cosmos that bring death and destruction are overcome with virtuous heroic action, unyielding optimism in a better world, or miraculous intervention. For Disney, who grew up under the stern hand of his father, a religious, working-class man who represented a disappearing world based on such Protestant values as hard work, sobriety, self-denial, and frugality, the emerging complex moral order of the universe could be depicted in paint by-number fashion. In the film *Fantasia* the association between death and evil is both unequivocal and at times quite surprising. According to Robert Fields, who wrote a tribute to the man in 1942, Disney made the following unpretentious comments about the setting for the "Night on Bald Mountain" sequence: "It sort of symbolizes something. The forces of good on one side and of evil on the other is what I'm trying to see in the thing. What other reason can there be for it?' (Feild: 122). As Jewett and Lawrence and others point out, this and other early Disney films show no interest in capturing the "moral gradations" in life (136; Culhane: 182).

His films depict a millennial vision of the universe, where absolute good battles with absolute evil, with death usually imagined as the result of evil intentions, or as a justified fate for the unredeemable. Jewett and Lawrence also identify a peculiar aspect of the personification of evil in many films—it is often linked with "curvaceous femininity": "The 'curves' of the wicked Queen are played off visually against the pure, straight lines of Snow White. A similar effort to associate curvaceous femininity with evil is made in 'Night on Bald Mountain,' where demonic hags are presented with bare breasts and extended nipples—the only occasion in Disney's film-making career for unveiling these menacing anatomic structures" (137). While Disney films promote obvious stereotypes relating to gender, the phallic symbolism of the demonic figure ruling over all the dark, fiendish activity is equally striking during this segment.

It is clear that the malevolent forces of evil are also associated with masculinity, or perhaps a "penetrating" masculinity. In one of Disney's most popular films Bambi's mother is killed by merciless hunters whose guns violate the pastoral innocence found in the forest. As one early critic playfully, and derogatorily, summarized the action of *Bambi* (1942): "The hero is a deer named Bambi, whose mother is killed by the villain, Mr Man, whose sweetheart is attacked by Mr Man's dogs, whose terrestrial paradise is destroyed by Mr Man's fire" (Farber: 90).

Evil comes in many forms in Disney films—man, stepmothers, bad fairies, curvaceous women, menacing whales, etc.—but whatever may cause the death, or insert the threat of death into the lives of the animated characters, the response is pure human pathos. In most cases, this response is depicted in the film itself. But in the special case of *Bambi* (1942) the profound emotional response is erased from the narrative in the fade to-black after the fawn confronts the reality of his mother's death. What contributes to the astonishing lingering power of this death scene in the lives of many Americans is the way in which the emotional weight is left for the audience to bear.

In his essay on Bambi, masculinity, and American hunting culture, David Payne identifies something shared by many Americans who have seen the film: "Bambi is often recalled as the most memorable film of peoples youth, not only for its charm and natural wonders, but because there children learned about death" (140). Although Bambi's mother is killed off camera, and the young fawn's response is blacked out, many in the audience experience the trauma, are impressed by its filmic reality and its depiction of a common childhood fear of permanent separation from the mother, and remember the moment for the rest of their lives. The community of feeling that usually forms on screen in the wake of death, or apparent death, is transferred in this film to the audience members watching together.

The experience of death as a profound, unacceptable rupture in the insulated world of the domestic family unit is a deeply-rooted cultural script that, according to Ariès, came to prominence in the nineteenth century (409-556). Ariès labels this culturally dominant attitude "the death of the other" and associates it with the emergence of the nuclear family, new forms of memorialization glorifying the irreplaceable individual, and valorization of the affections of the survivors. As the nuclear family came to represent a comforting, secure remedy to the chaos and danger found in the streets of late-nineteenth and early-twentieth-century America, the intrusion of death into home life brought the religious character of these bonds into sharp relief. Although absent from *Bambi*, the deathbed scene could also convey the sentimentality and holy anguish that erupts as grief at the sight of death. For example, in *Pinocchio* (1940), after Gepetto is saved from the whale by his creation and he places the deanimated puppet on the bed, the scene lingers on the heaving sobs of the gentle puppet maker and the dispirited countenance of Jimminy Cricket, the surrogate family whose lives have been enchanted—indeed given special meaning—by the presence of Pinocchio.

While Disney may have avoided funerals later in his life, he clearly understood the dramatic and commercial possibilities of the artfully illustrated deathbed scene. Transcripts from story conferences for the first, full-length animated film, *Snow White and the Seven Dwarfs* (1937),

125

capture Disney's awareness of these possibilities, as well as his energies and dominance in the creative process of producing films. Imagining the conclusion of the film, Disney articulates his vision of Snow White's encoffined body and the dwarfs' reactions to it:

> Fade in on her in the glass coffin, maybe shaded by a big tree. It's built on sort of a little pedestal, torches are burning, two dwarfs on either side with things like guards would have, others are coming up and putting flowers on the coffin. It's all decked with flowers. The birds fly up and drop flowers. Shots of the birds; show them sad. Snow White is beautiful in the coffin.
>
> Then you hear the Prince. The birds, dwarfs, everyone hear him offscreen. As they turn to look, here he is silhouetted against the hill with his horse. As he walks down the hill singing the song, cut to Snow White in the coffin. As he approaches, everyone sort of steps back as if he had a right there [sic]. He goes up to the coffin and finishes the song. As he finishes the song, he lifts the glass lid of the coffin and maybe there's a hesitation, then he kisses her. From the kiss he drops down and buries his head in his hands in a sad position, and all the dwarfs see it and every dwarf drops his head. (Thomas: 135-136)

The dwarfs foil the queen's plans by not burying the young woman alive. They, like many Americans in the first half of the twentieth century, were fixated on the beautiful body, too entranced by it to say goodbye forever, but unencumbered by professional managers whose job is to ensure the final separation between the living and the dead.

The joyful moments following the kiss that brings Snow White out of her "sleeping death" signal another element in the Disney way of death, an element that appears in all the films and contributes to their mythic power in American culture. That element, found in most religious systems as well, is, of course, the happy ending where death is not really the end but is defeated by the commendable main characters who live on in a safer, purified world. By the end of many Disney films, the threat of death is vanquished and, most importantly, the integrity of the family is reconstituted and made secure. After the death of Bambi's mother the advice of his father, the strong, dispassionate, wise Stag, is that he must carry on. The mourning and torment of losing a mother are hidden behind the black screen of time so that he can stoically make the transition from innocence to maturity. The rest of the movie follows Bambi's often difficult rite of passage into adulthood, where in the end he gets the girl. Payne remarks that the remainder of the film after the death encodes a certain type of sexual politics that relates to "Bambi's emergent masculinity discovered in combat, heroism, and survival, all of which are inspired, even manipulated by, his desire to win Faline for his mate (from the other deer) and to protect her from the ravages of survival (the evils of the hunters, the forest fire caused by invading 'Man')" (145).

In many Disney films death is a rite of passage for the individual hero that leads from, in many cases, an alternative, temporary, even broken family to the promise of living in the midst of an eternally loving, transcendent family unit — a model enshrined in various cultural expressions and publicly celebrated by a variety of religious institutions from the 1940s and 1950s on. We can see this commitment to a deep-rooted domestic religious ideology, and something of its millennial flavor, in the curse of the evil Maleficent, in the triumph of love after battling evil, and in the enactment of another death-defying kiss in *Sleeping Beauty* (1959). As in *Snow White*, the threat of death, or eternal sleep, imposed by a vain, powerful witch who does not have quite enough power to thwart the forces of good, inspires the actions of others to make sure the proper order of social life is not destroyed.

In *Pinocchio* it is clear that the puppet, not fully human and not quite the son Gepetto wishes for, spends most of the film in a dangerous environment where perverse adults are eager to kidnap and exploit the labor of donkey-children. As a result of his sacrificing his own life for the lives of others, the fairy sees that Pinocchio has learned his lesson and is worthy of her magic powers of resurrection. The dead puppet boy is then reborn as a real individual, securely and safely delivered into the hands of his creator and father, Gepetto. In the Disney imaginative universe, death can be overcome and serve as a source of regeneration because there are wondrous, supernatural forces in the universe that help us face our darkest fears: abandonment, disintegration, chaos. The vibrancy of American cultural religion depends in part on the potency of family relations and the desire to perpetuate the ties that bind individuals to a family unit, realities that are stronger and more powerful than the evil forces in the cosmos that conspire to destroy families. The idealized order presented in these fairy tales depicts moral teachings about the centrality of family in terms of gender roles, sexuality, the relation of the individual to the family, and the transition out of childhood.

In most of his films Disney ends the story with the promise of domestic bliss, a ray of hope in an uncertain, malevolent world. The fact that most of these films were released during a period in which American society as a whole was struggling with both national and international conflicts and relied on a variety of domestic symbols and images is not surprising. As Watts points out, a "Disney Doctrine" is the ideological driving force behind the man's vision, a doctrine that is essentially a recapitulation of dominant American values of the time, including the "notion that the nuclear family, with its attendant rituals of marriage, parenthood, emotional and spiritual instruction, and consumption, was the centerpiece of the American way of life" (326).

In many ways the Disney way of death is a critical reason the "Disney Doctrine" has so much cultural capital. As modern-day fairy tales, his films both reflect and shape religious sensibilities across the grain of American culture—they are popular meditations that rely on a cultural system of religious meanings to make sense of death. The centrality of death in these films mark them not only as significant cultural artifacts in the history of attitudes toward death in America but as revealing cultural texts that communicate popular fears about social disorder, common fantasies about family life as a source of transcendence, and idealistic dreams about American values and virtues. Without this preoccupation with death Disney would not have had the cultural impact he did in twentieth century America; if Americans in this period did not have similar preoccupations and similar strategies for imagining meaning in the face of death, his films would have held little public interest.

References

Ariès, Philippe 1982 *The Hour of Our Death.* Trans, by Helen Weaver. New York: Vintage.

Albanese, Catherine 1999 *America: Religions and Religion.* 3d ed. Belmont, CA: Wadsworth

Bell, Elizabeth, Lynda Haas, and Laura Sells, eds.1995 *From Mouse to Mermaid: The Politics of Film, Gender, and Culture.* Bloomington: Indiana University Press.

Bellah, Robert 1975 *The Broken Covenant: American Civil Religion in Time of Trial.* New York: Seabury Press.

Boyer, Paul 1992 *When Time Shall Be No More: Prophecy Belief in Modern America.* Cambridge, MA: Belknap Press.

Bryman, Alan 1995 *Disney and His Worlds.* London: Routledge.

Charmaz, Kathy 1980 *The Social Reality of Death: Death in Contemporary America.* New York: Random House.

Chidester, David 1996 "The Church of Baseball, the Fetish of Coca-Cola, and the Potlatch of Rock 'n' Roll: Theoretical Models for the Study of Religion in American Popular Culture." *Journal of the American Academy of Religion* 64/4 (Winter 1996): 743-765.

Churchill, Douglas W. 1938 "Disney's 'Philosophy.'" March 6: 9 and 22. *New York Times Magazine.*

Culhane, John 1983 *Walt Disney's Fantasia.* New York: Harry N. Abrams.

Darnton, Robert 1985 *The Great Cat Massacre and Other Stories in French Cultural History*. New York: Vintage.

DeSpelder, Lynne Ann, and Albert Lee Strickland 1999 *The Last Dance: Encountering Death and Dying*. Mountain View, CA: Mayfield.

Douglas, Ann 1988 *The Feminization of American Culture*. New York: Anchor Press.

Farber, Manny 1980 "Saccharine Symphony-Bambi!" In *The American Animated Cartoon: A Critical Anthology*. Ed. by Danny Peary and Gerald Peary. New York: E. P. Dutton.

Feifel, Herman, ed. 1959 *The Meaning of Death*. Preface and intro. by Herman Feifel. New York: McGraw Hill.

Feild, Robert D. 1942 T*he Art of Walt Disney*. New York: Macmillan.

Fulton, Robert, ed. 1965 *Death and Identity*. New York: Wiley.

Jackson, Kathy Merlock 1993 *Walt Disney: A Bio-Bibliography*. Westport, CT: Greenwood.

Jewett, Robert, and John Shelton Lawrence 1988 *The American Monomyth*. 2d ed. Lanham, MD: University Press of America.

Kübler-Ross, Elisabeth 1969 *On Death and Dying*. New York: Macmillan.

McDannell, Colleen 1996 *Material Christianity: Religion and Popular Culture in America*. New Haven, CT: Yale University Press.

McDannell, Colleen, and Bernhard Lang 1988 *Heaven: A History*. New Haven, CT: Yale University Press.

Moller, David Wendell 1996 *Confronting Death: Values, Institutions, and Human Mortality*. New York: Oxford University Press.

Mosley, Leonard 1985 *Disney's World: A Biography*. New York: Arno Press.

Payne, David 1995 "Bambi." In *From Mouse to Mermaid: The Politics of Film, Gender, and Culture*. Ed. by Elizabeth Bell et al. Bloomington: Indiana University Press.

Primiano, Leonard 1995 "Vernacular Religion and the Search for Method in Religious Folklife." *Western Folklore* 54: 37-56.

Pyles, Marian S 1988 *Death and Dying in Children's and Young People's Literature: A Survey and Bibliography*. Jefferson, NC: McFarland.

Schickel, Richard 1985 *The Disney Vision: The Life, Times, Art and Commerce of Walt Disney*. Rev. ed. New York: Simon and Schuster.

Sullivan, Lawrence, E., ed. 1989 *Death, Afterlife, and the Soul*. New York: Macmillan.

Tartar, Maria 1987 *The Hard Facts of the Grimms' Fairy Tales*. Princeton: Princeton University Press.

Thomas, Bob 1976 *Walt Disney: An American Original*. New York: Simon and Schuster.

Tucker, Nicholas 1968 "Who's Afraid of Walt Disney?" *New Society*, 288: 502-503.

Watts, Steven 1997 *The Magic Kingdom: Walt Disney and the American Way of Life*. Boston: Houghton Mifflin.

Willis, Susan, ed. 1993 "The World According to Disney." *South Atlantic Quarterly* 92/'1. Special Issue.

Published with permission from Oxford University Press. Gary Laderman, "The Disney Way of Death," Journal of the American Academy of Religion, v. 68, n. 1 (March 2000).

3.

Funereal Choices

"What do you want done with your body when you die?" This is a question I never fail to get from undergraduates in my college Death and Dying course. I've taught the class at Emory for roughly twenty years, and after a semester spent exploring attitudes toward death and mortuary practices over time and around the globe, students are most curious about this: the ultimate questions—not in theory, but in real life. My real life.

My answer is always playful and played to shock them. Depending on my mood, I might respond: "I'm planning to be embalmed, put in my best suit, and put on display in an open, ornate casket with beautiful flowers all around and lots of guests who will listen to my favorite music—the mournful tunes of Wilco, Uncle Tupelo, and Golden Smog." Or, if I'm feeling more macabre than normal, I'll say: "I'd like to stream my decaying corpse on my Facebook page. That way, as it's being eaten by vultures and other birds of prey, all of my friends can contemplate it, and better grasp the true realities of this physical body." Each time I get the question I usually mix it up. "Cremation and thrown to the wind is my preference," I might say; "unceremoniously buried in an unmarked grave in a natural setting" is another favorite as well, and quite popular at the moment.

What do you want done with your body when you die? What an incredible question. Incredible, but not because it is so personal and, dare I say, sacred. It's incredible in a different sense: I don't think that question is even possible to imagine, or has ever really been asked, throughout human history. Method of disposal of the body is not really a choice—you don't see many societies where individuals are given multiple options for disposition, or in which individuals make the decisions about their own corpses. Granted: the postmortem fates of the rich and powerful and the common folk are often not the same. But the very idea—what do you want done with your body?—is outside the conceptual realm of possibility in most of the world.

Funerary rituals are slow to change, they say. Through human history, available practices for disposing of the dead often remain stable; indeed, these practices are fundamental for conserving and maintaining social structures and power relationships. When the usual relations between the living and the dead are disrupted or abruptly transformed, it is likely that society is in the midst of dramatic upheaval and transformation.

In American history, the prevailing, dominant, deep-rooted model for human disposal was focused generally on two components: being present with the body before it disappears from society for good, and burying it in the ground. The details varied, but the results were the same: intimacy and proximity with the corpse, and internment in a churchyard or cemetery. The emergence of the funeral home in the later nineteenth and early twentieth century was spurred, in large part, by the Civil War and by the journey of Abraham Lincoln's preserved and displayed corpse at its end. The nascent funeral home in the later years of the nineteenth century only reified these elements, thanks to embalming and the commercialization of cemeteries. Differences in practice emerged throughout the twentieth century in terms of race and class, but the core remained the same. And no one was given a choice.

All that changed in the 1960s: a time of tremendous cultural crisis and instability, protests, and disruptions. Along with the general social convulsions and challenges to cultural authority, one book in particular catalyzed a change in the way Americans dispose of their dead: Jessica Mitford's *The American Way of Death*. Published in 1963, it opened the door for cremation and memorial societies to enter the public and private debates and deliberations on death rituals. More importantly, and in line with those times, Mitford's book empowered consumers to consider costs and personal preferences, delegitimizing traditional patterns tied to the two primary institutional authorities that had managed funeral rituals to that point: the church and the funeral industry. The book raised uncomfortable questions about the real value, meaning, and purpose of the corpse for the living.

Since then, many forces have conspired to turn the moment of death into a moment of consumption, enabling consumers to make choices about the most appropriate mode of disposal and the most fitting funeral rituals. Now more than ever, these mortuary practices are determined by the living, before they die, and not by family members and friends, after death. Throughout American history, American mortuary practices were determined by two (male) social groups: religious figures and undertakers/morticians/funeral directors after the Civil War. These two groups are now only two among many authorities on mortuary choices, and the traditions they used to maintain are losing ground; other traditions and innovations in corpse disposal are now on the market, and are available to an eager market of spiritually free consumers.

Members of the Baby Boomer generation are now the primary consumers of funeral goods and services for dying parents. They are also themselves getting closer to death, a demographic trend that will turn the Baby Boom into a Corpse Boon (a boon for the funeral industry, at least). The Boomers have always demanded choice, looking to customize their purchases to fit their lifestyles, personalities, and personal predilections. The high priests and role models in American popular culture, celebrities and entertainment idols, also have assumed an even greater role in shaping attitudes and legitimating practices at the time of death, providing the public a new range of possibilities for what can and can't be done with the dead in the second half of the twentieth and beginnings of the twenty-first centuries.

Finally, the millennials have now arrived on the scene in the wake of the Boomers, and are increasingly identified as "nones," (individuals unaffiliated with any particular religion but who are religious and spiritual in other ways). Their presence will surely only reinforce these trends — moving away from "traditional" American funerals and toward rituals with a more democratic, consumer-driven, and experimental sensibility.

What do the mortuary practices of a society tell us about that society? Why do the living care about the postmortem fate of the body? Does the treatment of the corpse have a bearing on how the dead are remembered? Are these religious questions? Ethical? Economic? The American way of death is, in many ways, a mirror of the American way of life, celebrating sacred values associated with individualism, free choice, and spiritual innovation and experimentation. In recent times, traditions have been losing ground; sources of authority about the dead body, and the ultimate meaning of death, have been shifting and diversifying. These changes in American mortuary customs speak volumes about religious and cultural realities in America today.

Originally published in Cosmologics, a magazine of science, religion, and culture through the Science, Religion, and Culture Program at Harvard Divinity School, 2015

4.

Mortality Now: Top 5 Reminders Of Death For Aging Baby Boomers

Memento Mori. Remember, you will die. Not a pleasant thought, yet one that has universal application because it is an unavoidable truth. The vanity of life, the nature of impermanence, the transient quality of existence. You get the point. These are only a few of the sentiments associated with recognizing one's mortality. We in the west might be more familiar with the visual signs and symbols bringing death to mind in European Christian art: an hourglass, a skull, or perhaps the appearance of the Grim Reaper himself. And make no mistake, many religions around the world and through time understand how reflections on death bring life to spirituality, moral order, and ultimate meanings.

In America, what spurs our reflections on death, and helps us recognize the reality of one's own death? How does today compare with the past? I've written a couple of books on the history of death in America, particularly focusing on the nineteenth and twentieth centuries, and have been wondering more and more about what has changed, and what remains the same. Before the Civil War Americans were quite intimate with the realities of death. Mortality rates were dramatically different than today—likely impossible for us to even imagine. Not only higher infant mortality rates, shorter life spans, greater impact from diseases and infections, and so on, but community and family structures ensured that the death of relations and neighbors was a familiar dimension of everyday life. Death and the dead were part of the American landscape, common features in private letters, public discourse, and the popular imagination.

After the Civil War, the death scene changes—is indeed, radically transformed. The birth of funeral homes and modern hospitals help to take death, or some aspects of death, out of sight and out of the hands of family members and relations. Advances in medicine and public health are part and parcel of a modern attitude that emerges that is tied, in large part, to the rise of science and the decline of theology as key touchstones during the transition from dying to dead, and in answering the question about what to do with the corpse. Mortality rates improve, people begin to live longer, and the nuclear family replaces the larger and more communal ties of extended family. In most of the country, the intimacy with death that existed before the Civil War was long gone by the early decades of the twentieth century.

It's in the middle decades of the twentieth century that many social scientists and social commentaries begin to argue that Americans "deny" the reality of death, and that the topic is "taboo" in public settings—conditions that were ripe for an array of specialists and experts to talk endlessly about and study death. Contributing to these unhealthy cultural attitudes, these critics claim, are the very institutions that gained supreme authority over death and dying at the turn of the century. In the hospital death is a defeat, a failure on the part of the doctors who could not "save" the patient from the worst fate imaginable for Americans who dream of staying forever young. In the funeral home, the practice of embalming and presenting the corpse is the main culprit that so clearly and categorically hides the reality of death from loved ones, according to the critics.

Whether or not you buy these assertions about American culture in the twentieth century, it is hard to deny that the experience of death — its frequency in everyday life and the impact of losing and then burying a loved one — is quite different than before the Civil War. Many Americans growing up in the middle of the twentieth century struggled with the death of a pet or the death of a grandparent, significant moments in the life of an individual for sure that pack a punch and make a mark. Over the second half of the twentieth century and especially with the baby boomers born in the 1950s and 60s, things changed, dramatically, in terms of mortality rates, consumer empowerment, religious identities and identifications, celebrity culture, social media, and so on.

So what are the signs and symbols for aging baby boomers that bring death to mind? When and how are we called upon to remember the reality of our own mortality? There's only one way to answer these questions: with a top five list, of course.

5. NO ESCAPE FROM HEALTH CARE CULTURE: Let's say straight up that these promptings are not coming from the dominant religion in the country, Christianity, which is too concerned with politics, prosperity, and power to delve into the deeper, more profound questions about mortality. Instead, the dominant force shaping the encounter with death is health care culture. End of life care and other issues are integrally bound up with medical science whether you are looking to extend life or extinguish it on one's own terms. There is nothing to get you thinking realistically about your own death like imagining the fate of many Americans who die enmeshed in and at the mercy of hospital conglomerates, pharmaceutical companies, and health care professionals.

4. OLDER PARENTS, DYING: Most of us are now witnessing or have recently witnessed the death of our parents. Of course that is nothing unusual. Parents have died throughout history. But over the course of the

second half of the twentieth and into the early years of the twenty-first century, longevity has improved, and parents have generally been living longer. So for many baby boomers, the profoundly personal and powerful experience of watching parents die is now occurring in middle and later middle age. In many ways, the boomers have not been adequately prepared for this passage, and now whether it is tragically or peacefully finished, the loss of a parent is a mortality wake up call.

3. THANK GOD FOR DEATH EXPERTS: Fortunately, a bubbling consumer industry is helping us all prepare and plan for death. Books, magazine articles, ads, social media — just about everywhere you look these days you will find so called experts who have the know-how, skills, and training to make your reflections on mortality more informed and practical. Do-it-yourself funerals? There are professionals to help with that. Planning a living will or for a more humane way to deal the hospice care? Guidebooks and scholarly monographs are abundant for purchase to consumers who want to know about death. As much as we think reflecting on death is a solitary endeavor, this efflorescence of publishing and practical guides suggests a more collectively directed activity is going on.

2. THAT'S ENTERTAINMENT: Popular cultures teach us stories about death — what it means, how to cope, why it happens, even where the spirit goes. I'm not sure there's a more potent and pervasive source for reminding Americans of mortal matters than entertainment. The lists are too easy to compile: from the death of Bambi's mother to Johnny Depp's film *Transcendence*; from Pink Floyd's "Time" to Bone Thugs-n-Harmony,'s "Crossroads"; from Edith Bunker's death in *All in the Family* to Hank Schrader's death in *Breaking Bad*, popular cultures are saturated with reminders of death, even though the moral messages and social meanings conveyed in this arena are far from unanimous.

1. MORE CELEBRITY DEATHS ON THE WAY: The top spot for influencing our own sense of mortality are the real-life deaths of celebrities. The recent deaths of David Bowie and Glenn Frey, and the more distant ones like Robin Williams, or Tupac, or Princess Diana, all point to one clear trend: celebrity deaths make a huge impact on fans and fan cultures, and their increasing frequency (and let's face it, the number of celebrities has skyrocketed over the last 50 years) will only enhance the vitality of fame in American culture. It seems to me it is the death of celebrities that is bringing back a certain kind of intimacy with death that makes it familiar, and this in turn spurs on Americans not only to feel the sting of death, but also reflect on it with more vigor and, dare I say, sacred creativity.

Originally published in the Huffington Post, 2016.

5.

Suicide: The Last Taboo?

Who wants to talk about suicide? I'll tell you who: young students in the range of 18 to 22, the very age group in which suicide has lately become one of the leading causes of death. How do we as a society address this startling, and startlingly tragic, new trend among young people? Who can they turn to to openly and directly talk with about their feelings and thoughts on a subject that hits so close to home for so many of them?

Is suicide the last taboo in our society? Historically, we often look at the Victorian era in the later nineteenth century as a time when public discussion of sex was considered "taboo"; for much of the twentieth century, some argue, death replaced sex as the great taboo operating in our culture. Today I doubt that anything can be considered taboo. We talk about the size and look of the president's private parts; pornography is mainstream; violence and graphic depictions of carnage in video games and films are ubiquitous and celebrated; incest, pedophilia, cannibalism...it's all out there and available for public consumption, so to speak.

I have been reading about suicide statistics lately and some of the stories of young people taking their own lives, but even these reports do not seem to open up and explore what is going on in our society that is contributing to this new reality about death in the lives of so many. Yes, some people blame social media, or the time younger folks spend on their phones, or skyrocketing rates of depression and mental illness in that population, or the lack of strong religious grounding in their lives, and so on. Yet somehow it seems we are not really fully confronting and discussing suicide with the very people who are most at risk, but rather talking at them and not listening.

Now I know suicide is a big topic. When a soldier sacrifices their own life to save the lives of others, that is a hero. For an aged person who has lived a long life, and whose quality of life is so diminished and tortured, ending life on your own terms might be considered for some the more humane, morally sensible action to take. In general, the notion that some people, in some circumstances, may see taking their own life as an ethically sound, psychologically reasonable thing to do, opens a door that many prefer to keep closed. When we are talking about older children and young adults killing themselves, however, reasonable arguments and exceptions to the rule are unacceptable.

What are the cultural scripts and conceptual frames that shape public discourse about suicide? Suicide is certainly in the news, and one of the ways Americans collectively reflect on its presence in society is in the case of celebrity suicides, when we all wonder how people with money, success, and fame would choose death over life. Recently, and a sign that things are changing I think, the band The 1975 released an album called *A Brief Inquiry Into Online Relationships* which includes the song "I Always Want to Die (Sometimes)." In a brief video interview, Matthew Healey, the lead singer, discusses the meaning of the song, and speaks directly about the prevalence of thinking about suicide in our society these days.

On the one hand, across the board religions are deeply and strongly opposed to suicide. While I try to stay away from over-generalizations, I think it's safe to say that in principle for most religious cultures life is sacred, the taking of life including one's own is a supreme moral violation, and historically at least, it has been understood that suicide can impact your status in the afterlife. So for many in religious communities, suicide can represent a moral weakness or a spiritual failure within the individual; or that evil, malevolent forces may have corrupted and influenced the individual.

On the other hand, throughout American culture the easy fall back explanation for suicide is to apply medical labels, raise the flag of mental illness, and identify the internal or external factors that led to the psychological breakdown (depression, genetics, side-effects from other drugs, and so on). The suicide in this sense becomes an exemplary case demonstrating the need for more psychological treatment that often, maybe always, looks to prescription drugs to tweak cognitive and neurological processes in order to restore "mental balance," whatever that is.

My own personal, unscientific intuition is that both of these conceptual frames are not helpful to having open, honest, and challenging conversations about suicide among this age group. I teach at a university so am keenly aware of rising rates of suicides among college age kids. But even more importantly, and closer to home, I teach a Death and Dying class that enrolls about 200 students. To be honest, over the twenty years or so I've been teaching the class I have stayed away from the topic of suicide, though I do always enjoy mentioning the famous book, *The Sorrows of Young Werther*, written by the German Romantic Johann Wolfgang von Goethe, which supposedly created a strange outbreak of copycat suicides based on the story. Other than that, it has been, well, taboo in my class.

Something happened this semester that has never happened before in all my years teaching the course. I have had now several students come in and tell me they have faced the realities of suicide as a result of classmates and others close to them who killed themselves or

145

attempted to kill themselves. I am just a professor, not a religious leader nor a therapist. My class is an academic, intellectual space for students to learn about death across cultures, throughout history, and in American society. It is not, at least on the surface, a space for existential or therapeutic self-exploration, or for personal religious or spiritual discovery.

In all of these private conversations, as delicate, emotional, and difficult as they have been, students have mentioned that whenever adults have attempted to talk with them about suicide—the special teams of counselors and/or religious leaders who come in to schools after a suicide has occurred to help students cope with the experience; the specialized therapists and mental health professionals who spring into action when a young person tries to take their own life—it has been ineffective. These older children and young adults claim they were not really heard, that they were unable to articulate fully what they experienced, how they were feeling, and what they were thinking.

Many of these students want to talk about suicide but cannot seem to find the right context. Conversations can be difficult with family members; social settings with friends doesn't quite work well; religious leaders and professionals seem to have their own presuppositions and conceptual limitations on the topic. So where to go and who to talk to about this most pressing, life and death topic? I am still hesitant to pursue it in my class—perhaps because of the feeling that it is "taboo"; perhaps because a lingering sense that only "professionals" should be talking about it. It is highly, highly charged for so many of us. As one student put it, "trigger warnings were made for this topic."

The numbers of young people killing themselves is astonishing and points to larger cultural and social problems that we all should be concerned about for America's future. As a professor who tackles the topic of death in all of its fascinating, revealing dimensions, and loves to entertain and enlighten students, I am stumped and uncertain about this topic and how, or if, I should address it in class. It is clear from my meetings with students that for many—not all—a neutral, intellectually open and honest context for discussing suicide is sorely needed.

Originally published in Sacred Matters, 2018.

6.

The Dead are With Us

The dead are with us. At least that's what most religious cultures tell us. In some form or other, the living remember the dead, whether it is one special figure who binds a community, like Jesus, or the more amorphous, but still community forming, collective of ancestors who serve as the focal point of living memory. In so many religious cultures the fate of the living and the fate of the dead are intermingled and intimately connected, and the care and concern from either side can have monumental effects on all.

Ritual, a core element in any religious culture, helps to structure the interactions between the spirits of the dead and the actions of the living, ordering objects in space, defying the passage of time, and communicating messages about morality and values to participants and observers. Throughout human history, rituals for the dead have been integral to social order and cultural meanings, bearing on the emotional and psychological state of the living and unifying a community around shared identities and purposes.

The Lantern Floating Ceremony, held every Memorial Day in Honolulu, Hawaii, for the last twenty years by the Shinnyo-en school of contemporary esoteric Buddhism, is an illustrative example of these ritual elements, but also a splendid expression of the many cultural forces shaping how the living relate to the dead in the second half of the twentieth century and into the early decades of the twenty-first. I had the privilege of participating in and observing the event this year, a serendipitous invitation that caught both my scholarly interest as someone who has spent a career researching death and religion, and my personal interest as a son who had just lost his mother over a year earlier.

Many components of the experience stand out in my memory, and they were particularly fascinating for someone who pays attention to and studies changing attitudes and practices surrounding death in America. Beyond simply the beauty of the beach location where all this took place, some of the scenes from the day also radiated beauty, and power, and profound emotional energies. Indeed, the overall impact of the ceremony left a strong impression on me as I found myself both identifying and empathizing with those living with loss, and analyzing and critiquing the collective representations of death at work in the spectacular scene all around me.

The draw of the ceremony for others was evident even before it began. Long lines of people early in the morning were waiting to enter tents where they would construct the floating lanterns that later in the evening are sent out for the spirits of the dead, bearing their personal messages. On the calming waters of the ocean bay, the living will use lanterns as a medium for some form of communication, connection, or communion with the spirits who will, we all hope, receive, read, and be liberated by those messages. Many in line were pilgrims who traveled from other parts of the world to be at this annual ritual; but a great many were local Hawaiians, a cultural presence in all aspects of the ritual, it seemed to me, and a force shaping the tone and texture of this Buddhist ceremony.

In addition to the long and winding lines that stretched across parts of Ala Moana Beach Park were the groups of people setting up camp on the beach in the early morning before the evening ceremony. Small tents, umbrellas, ice chests, towels and blankets, grills, American flags—what anyone would expect on Memorial Day in anywhere in the US of A—in between the looming remains of a volcanic eruption that took place hundreds of thousands of years ago, now known as Diamond Head, and the Pearl Harbor memorial site. What struck me here were the number of personal memorials to deceased family members and friends—flags and banners flying in memory of the dead, usually containing an image or picture of the person who died, life dates, brief sentiments of love, and so on. One was a large banner hanging from an elaborate awning that read "Grandpa & Grandma, Together Forever, July 17, 2017" and included photos of the couple from throughout their lives, together; another had images of a woman, including one with angel wings incorporated into the image, with the woman's name and life dates, and the words "An angel in need, is an angel indeed" and "Rest in Peace, Our Angel."

By the start of the ceremony around 7:30pm, over 50,000 people from Hawaii, the US mainland, Japan, Australia, France, and across the globe, congregated and waited in the warmth—sometimes with clouds and rain blowing in and out—of the relatively small strip of beach. Out of that 50,000, 7,000 or so were waiting to send their personalized, or in some cases collectively designed, lanterns into the relatively still waters. The ceremony itself is in its twentieth year, a fitting and illustrative expression of key components of this particular brand of modern Buddhism but also, in its way, an encapsulation of 21st century trends in American public religious death and mourning rituals.

The rich, vibrant mixing of different cultural elements in the setting, staging, words, music, performance, objects, and people highlighted during the ceremony before the release of the lanterns was anchored in a distinctive Shinnyo-en religious cultural cosmology. But I also suspect there were other religious cosmologies at work here, though not in conflict with or challenging to the sacred esoteric Buddhist notions

151

animating this service, but in harmony with them, or at least apparently in harmony. Here we have, at one level, an image of multiple religious cultures cohering and integrating in common action, in stark contrast with the more common historically-rooted public image of religions in mortal combat over politics and fear.

Over the course of the ceremony, a vibrant mixture of religious cultures surfaced and captured my attention as both a participant in the middle of all this vibrancy and effervescence, and a scholar who works with a broad-based conceptualization of religion and what might count as sacred, especially when it comes to the topic and experiences of death. Hawaiian political leaders and indigenous leaders and musical performers were singled out and shared the stage, tapping into and integrating local sacred sources of pride and identity. Religious leaders from local communities, including Muslims, Hindus, Jews, Catholics, Protestants, and other representatives participated in and were identified from the stage, displaying the interfaith fabric that is growing more complex and diverse in American public life in the twenty-first century. The centrality of the American military presence in Hawaii, a surprising and commanding element in the ceremony, surfaced in the introduction of key military leaders and the repeated reminders to remember the sacrifices of American soldiers (an element that should not be surprising at all given the occasion of the ceremony, the American holiday Memorial Day, which is so closely associated with war and military death). Media played a substantial role in the ceremony, with large monitors transmitting images in real-time of ritual events on stage, individual grieving faces from the hundreds lining the beaches, and lanterns floating out to sea, all combining to help generate and sustain the sacred energies and hopes for those present in the flesh, but also via online mechanisms allowing for virtual but very real participation and engagement with the activities. Finally, but most importantly, is the authorial and authorizing Shinnyo-en Buddhist religious culture, which provides the historical roots, ritual frameworks, and mythological touchstones through which all of this transpires and succeeds.

Each of these religious threads can be disentangled from the others and studied on their own; and all of the threads together has its own unique sociological and cultural significance that bears on the present. But whatever the approach or focus when writing and reflecting back on the event, the Lantern Floating ceremony presents a unique and compelling phenomenon for further consideration. These intellectual stirrings and comments about my own participation in the ceremony and observations about it, however, have not yet touched on the most impressive and moving experience during my time that evening. It was not, I must admit, putting my own lantern in the water for my mother and watching it, with my own inept attempt at words to connect us, floating out with thousands of others into the ocean at sunset in one of the more gorgeous locations on earth. No, it was rather when I turned around, away from the flickering lights and orange sky reflecting on the water, and toward the seated audience of hundreds behind me in a section on the beach with a view of lanterns floating on the sea.

As soon as my sight shifted from my feet on the shore walking out of the water to the faces of those seated under bright white lights for the cameras, I was taken aback and startled, and then tremendously touched by what I saw. Almost everyone seated on the chairs was Asian and over sixty, and it looked like every single one of them had tears in their eyes. This is obviously based on the immediate impression and memory of the moment, not on any surveys or statistical data. But the initial emotional impact hit me hard and left me feeling more tuned in to their sadness and experiences there than my own.

I could not take my eyes off of the group so brightly lit in front of me, but also knew that I was uncomfortable gazing in their direction as I walked away from the crowds on the beach. Even as lanterns floated in a picturesque, sunset setting, including my own to my dear and sorely

153

missed mother, my empathy and intellectual curiosity focused on these more elderly people sitting near the beach—with many actually leaning in toward the water on their right. The thoughts that jumped to mind centered around questions like: Who are they, and why are they there? And why is this so sad for them? With more time to reflect on the individuals in those chairs, and greater distance from the vivid moment itself, I find myself especially curious about whether the ceremony was sacred for them and if so, how so—and do their religious experiences line up at all with any of the religious cultures in the mix I sketched earlier? Are they memorializing individual family and friends who have died, ancestors from distant generations, lost cultural traditions no longer viable in the US, deceased Shinnyo-en community members, American military heroes who have died for the nation, or maybe even those who died as a result of American military force.

Beyond the particularities that well-studied answers might provide to these sorts of questions, that get into the minutiae of lived experiences or the fine-grained analysis of survey and demographic data for example, is something simple, shared, and systemic in all human cultures that is found in this profound event and elemental in the collective emotional energies generating the spiritual insights, connections, and experiences of participants: the dead remain present among the living and bind them together in various imagined but real social formations like family, nation, religion, culture, ethnicity, humanity, and so on. The deep and real pain of losing someone you love, not only those in old age but certainly when death strikes the young, does not go away, and the longer one lives, the more familiar one becomes to death's striking presence and impact, and the growing number of dead spirits that inhabit, and haunt, our worlds. It is unnecessary to state the obvious, but the experience with death does truly raise the most vital, fundamental, ultimate questions for individuals, including the more socially oriented ones, such as "who are my people, with whom do I belong, who will I be with after I die?"

154

The Lantern Floating ceremony puts this foundational intimacy with the dead on display in a way that explicitly communicates the long and deep-rooted human tendency to keep the dead close by. It also subtly performs a local intervention on this beach in Hawaii to remind all those present and participating, either in person or virtually, that across many social divisions, in the face of local histories replete with power struggles and conflict, and with the hope of bringing relief from suffering and cultivating compassion, the dead have a role to play. The religious cultures present at the ceremony do not simply coexist; they coalesce around the dead—the potency of memories, the crush that comes with grief, the solace from communing with ancestors, the desire for maintaining their presence—in ways that make the ritual so potent and effective. It strikes at the heart of individual participants, who are there for any number of reasons, who bring with them whatever spiritual resources and traditions work to connect them with the dead, and who by being involved in the ritual mix, virtually or in the flesh on the beach, can potentially reestablish communities that transcend and incorporate the realities of death.

Originally published in the booklet, Floating Lantern Hawaii: 2018, written at the invitation of the Center for Information on Religion, Shinn-yo-en Foundation.

Afterword:

Thinking About Death in Pandemic Times

Death in American life has changed dramatically in the several months since I finished writing this memoir on mortality. The pandemics of 2020, one fueled by the mysterious COVID-19 virus, the other fueled by the all-too-familiar racism embedded in American society, have transformed the landscapes of death through which we are making this journey of life.

At this point, close to 150,000 Americans have died from the virus, a dose of mass death by common cause in an amazingly short period of time that is public knowledge for all to see, but which affects Americans differently. What do we think about mass death in our pandemic present? What "we" think depends no doubt in part on age, religious perspective, social community affiliations, political party, media choices, and so on.

Death in the abstract—communicated through numbers or media reports—is only one side of this new landscape. The traditional settings and communities involved in dying are unsettled and highly regulated now. Forms of human intimacy so critical at the moment of death in most societies are being denied to sequestered and isolated COVID-19 patients dying in hospitals. Material corpses, and the disposal and funereal challenges now posed by these still-sacred remains, will bring to life new forms of ritual and memorialization, as well as new considerations about the significance and meaningfulness of the lifeless body to the living community.

I'd like to think, as Shakespeare once wrote, "what's past is prologue," and my expertise in the history of death and funerals might help shed some light on how the landscape will look into the future. But I am not so sure that what is behind us will have any bearing on what's ahead.

Mass death is one thing, but the video of the slow and horrific death of one individual at the cruel hands of the police is something else entirely. The death of George Floyd in Minneapolis, Minnesota, in March, 2020, ignited and catalyzed what some argue may become the largest ongoing social protest movement in US history.

Floyd's death, however, is not singular. He is one of many, many African Americans killed by the police and others whose deaths were not justified and whose names — Breonna Taylor, Ahmaud Arbery, Atatiana Jefferson, Rayshard Brooks, Elijah McClain — evoke both outrage and ritual commemorations that are having and will continue to have sacred reverberations in American culture. Their names, and the religious rituals of protest and reparations, are bringing the dead back to life and consciousness, and forcing us Americans to reckon with the deep-seeded blood, violence, and carnage tied to racism in America's past and present.

The essential problem today remains the same as always in all human cultures: how do we live with the dead? Again, the "we" is important, simultaneously encompassing me, a human being like all humans who must face and make sense of mortality and knows, along with Jim Morrison of The Doors, at a fundamental level of knowledge that "no one gets out of here alive." The "we" also includes me as an individual, personally missing my mom still, thinking of and imagining conversations with Luís, still mourning the deaths of people I've never met, like Sandra Bland, or Tom Petty. Finally, the "we" also includes me as a member of social groups and subcultures, and who reacts and interacts with collective representations of death and memories of the dead—an American who wants to tear down Confederate monuments and all memorial celebrations of the Confederacy; or, an academic who engages in various forms of ancestor worship within my field of Religious Studies and loves to channel the ghosts of Durkheim or Freud.

It is too bad that this "essential problem" that we all share, the universal, undeniable, indisputable, ubiquitous reality of death and living with the dead, does not lead to more compassion, love, sympathy, caring, and empathy, qualities that are sorely lacking in any meaningful way in American society today, a time of plagues and disunion.

Let's face it, the Grim Reaper has always been unjust, political, brutal, swift, selective, poignant, and unfair. Yes, Death is the "great equalizer" and comes to us all, for sure, but sometimes, in some moments of monumental historical import, mass death and shameful deaths can inspire dramatic social transformations that follow in the aftermath. Joe Strummer, lead singer for The Clash, who died in his early 50s, once said, "the future is unwritten," an apt sentiment for our current, unstable present, when the past does seem more and more like a distant, fading memory, though haunting us all with reminders and glimpses of what has been lost, and what's ahead is uncharted territory, a foreign country where things will be done differently than before the pandemics.

It might contradict the literal words in the title of this book, but what might help us and refresh American society now more than ever, is robust and deep reflection on mortality. In other words: think about death. I can confess that slightly obsessing about death and its reality does not only have to be morbid and depressing—it can also be quite liberating, illuminating, and humanizing, even in disturbing pandemic times like these.

Gary Laderman is Goodrich C. White Professor of American Religious History and Cultures at Emory University. He is the author of *The Sacred Remains: American Attitudes Toward Death, 1799–1883*, *Rest in Peace: A Cultural History of Death and the Funeral Home in 20th Century America*, and *Sacred Matters: Celebrity Worship, Sexual Ecstasies, the Living Dead, and Other Signs of Religious Life in the United States*.